MUSIC EXPRESS

YEAR 7

B **K 3** MUSICAL CYCLES
(WEST AFRICA)

Se   vised by
M: Hanke

Bo   mpiled by
En   eler

wit   th Bray
an   tephens

A&   ON

BOOK CONTENTS

Introduction 4

About *Music Express Year 7* 5

Musical cycles (West Africa): outline 10

LESSON 1 Rhythmic skills 12

LESSON 2 Signals and polyrhythms 20

LESSON 3 Melody and song 28

LESSON 4 Starting to compose 34

LESSON 5 Developing and rehearsing 42

LESSON 6 Bringing it all together 48

Djolé: dunun cyclic patterns 52

Djolé: signal and djembé cyclic patterns 53

Glossary 54

Acknowledgements 56

AUDIO CD TRACK LIST

TRACK	CONTENT	TRACK	CONTENT
1	Basic four-beat body percussion rhythms	21	All three simplified *Djolé* dunun rhythms + signal
2	Harder four-beat body percussion rhythms	22	Full djembé accompaniment 1
3	Eight-beat body percussion rhythms	23	Full djembé accompaniment 2
4	Copy track: full *Djolé* dununba rhythm	24	Full djembé accompaniments 1 and 2 together
5	Copy track: full *Djolé* sangban rhythm	25	Simplified djembé accompaniment 1
6	Copy track: full *Djolé* kenkeni rhythm	26	Simplified djembé accompaniment 2
7	Copy track: simplified *Djolé* dununba rhythm	27	Simplified djembé accompaniments 1 and 2 together
8	Copy track: simplified *Djolé* sangban rhythm	28	Improvisation by Mamady Keïta
9	Copy track: simplified *Djolé* kenkeni rhythm	29	Call and response signal
10	Extract of *Djolé* performed by Mamady Keïta and his troupe, Sewa Kan	30	Copy track: *Laïlaïko* phrases
11	Signal	31	*Laïlaïko* sung with gaps for responses
12	Full *Djolé* dununba rhythm + signal	32	*Laïlaïko* sung in harmony
13	Full *Djolé* sangban rhythm + signal	33	Call and response rhythm
14	Full *Djolé* kenkeni rhythm + signal	34	Extract of *Kayi ni wura* by Oumou Sangaré
15	Full *Djolé* dununba and sangban rhythms + signal	35	Melodic improvisation: extract of *Kayi ni wura* by Oumou Sangaré
16	All three full *Djolé* dunun rhythms + signal	36	Tobias Stürmer explains his reorchestration of the rhythm piece, *Djembé jam*
17	Simplified *Djolé* dununba rhythm + signal	37	Tobias Stürmer's reorchestration of his rhythm piece, *Djembé funk* – performance
18	Simplified *Djolé* sangban rhythm + signal		
19	Simplified *Djolé* kenkeni rhythm + signal		
20	Simplified *Djolé* dununba and sangban rhythms + signal		

CD-ROM CONTENTS

PRESENTATION

Unit overview
Learning intentions lessons 1–6

PRINTOUTS

1 Unit overview
2 Maps of West Africa
3 Notes to accompany video clip 1
4 Learning intentions lessons 1–6
5 Rhythm grid for *Djolé* dunun cyclic patterns
6 Background information: dunun drums
7 West African popular musicians
8 Rhythm grid for *Djolé* djembé cyclic patterns
9 Djembé teaching tips
10 Lyric sheet: *Laïlaïko*
11 *Laïlaïko* melody
12 Background information: *Kayi ni wura*
13 *Kayi ni wura*: notation and suggestions
14 Key words
15 *Laïlaïko* melody: keyboard
16 *Kayi ni wura*: notation and suggestions – keyboard
17 Pupils' guide to using Audacity
18 Performance cards
19 Composition assessment criteria
20 Performance assessment criteria
21 Notation ideas
22 Writing ideas down
23 Homework: ideas for rhythm piece
24 End of unit evaluation sheet

VIDEO CLIPS

1 Everyday life and music in Senegal
2 Reference: body percussion rhythm patterns
3 Reference: body percussion cyclic patterns
4 Extract of *Djolé*
5 Reference: learning dunun rhythms for *Djolé*
6 *Djolé* performed on classroom percussion
7 *Djolé* performance
8 *Djembé jam*: starting to compose
9 Developing your starting point
10 Building a structure
11 *Djembé funk* by Tobias Stürmer
A-E Full dunun parts for *Djolé*
F-J Simplified dunun parts for *Djolé*
K Signal
L-N Full djembé parts for *Djolé*
O-Q Simplified djembé parts for *Djolé*

PICTURE GALLERY

Djembés
Dununs
Other West African drums
Hand-held percussion

AUDACITY FILES

4beat1.wav	kenfull.wav	dje1simp.wav
4beat2.wav	dunsimp.wav	dje2simp.wav
8beat.wav	sansimp.wav	wawako.wav
pulse.wav	kensimp.wav	aiya.wav
dunfull.wav	dje1full.wav	lailaiko.wav
sanfull.wav	dje2full.w	

TEACHER INFORMATION

Sample lesson plan
Using ICT
Using electronic keyboards
Using Audacity
Using this CD-ROM

First published 2005
by A&C Black Publishers Ltd
38 Soho Square, London W1D 3HB
© 2005 A&C Black Publishers Ltd
ISBN 10: 0-7136-7364-8
ISBN 13: 978-0-7136-7364-7

Teaching text © 2005 Emily Keeler, Elizabeth Bray and John Stephens
CD/CD-ROM compilation © ℗ 2005 A&C Black
Edited by Emily Wilson, Abigail Walmsley and Harriet Lowe
Inside design by James Watson, Susan McIntyre, Jocelyn Lucas and
Carla Moss. Cover design by Jocelyn Lucas
CD-ROM interface design by Tatiana Demidova
Cover illustration © 2005 Graham Hutchings
Inside illustrations © 2005 Kanako Damerum and Yuzuru Takasaki
Music setting by Jeanne Roberts
Audio CD recording by John Boham-Cook; sound engineering by Tobias
Stürmer

Video clips filmed by Jamie Acton-Bond at AB Video Productions and
Landing Mané; edited by Jamie Acton-Bond at AB Video Productions
CD-ROM post-production by Ian Shepherd and Karen Manning at
Sound Recording Technology

A&C Black uses paper produced with elemental chlorine-free pulp,
harvested from managed sustainable forests.

INTRODUCTION

Musical cycles (West Africa) is the third of six units in *Music Express Year 7*. It combines performing, composing and listening activities to explore the structures and key characteristics of both traditional and modern West African music.

This half term unit of work is divided into six coherent and clearly structured lessons. Each lesson is 50 minutes long (with extension activities for schools with more time available) and progresses in a controlled and challenging way.

Pupils will be introduced to West African instruments, music and its context through video clips, workshop-style activities and listening. Pupils complete a composition or performance task and are able to consider the strengths of their work against the clearly described objectives. The composition element can be explored through the use of acoustic instruments, electronic keyboards or ICT and is modelled by a professional composer in the video clips on the CD-ROM.

Activities and resources are provided for using acoustic instruments, electronic keyboards and ICT, as suits the needs and set-up of each school.

The activities are described in the book; the CD and CD-ROM provide all the supporting material and resources needed for each lesson.

ABOUT THE SERIES AUTHOR

Maureen Hanke MA BMus is the head of Norfolk Education Service. She started her career as a music teacher in the East End of London. Later, as a music adviser, she developed a national reputation for music education workshops and became Head of Music Education at Trinity College of Music. Her work has involved PGCE training, QCA consultation and more recently she devised *Music Express*, an award-winning school resource.

ABOUT THE AUTHORS OF MUSICAL CYCLES (WEST AFRICA)

Emily Keeler MA BEd works currently as an Advanced Skills Teacher for primary music within Wandsworth Schools Music Service and is also the founder of Sewa-education, a charity providing West African music and dance education programmes. Over the last seven years she has researched and explored methods of teaching and learning West African music with young people in the UK and in West Africa, team-teaching with West African musicians and also teaching djembé at Key Stage 3. She is the author of several articles on West African music education and has worked extensively with secondary teacher trainees.

Elizabeth Bray worked for several years as Head of Music at Daventry William Parker School before taking up the post of Advanced Skills Teacher for Music at The Priory LSST in Lincoln, where she is also involved in county initiatives. She has written several articles on music education and worked as an OFSTED inspector.

John Stephens has taught music at all levels for almost twenty years in the London boroughs of Greenwich, Lewisham and Southwark. He has also produced music commercially, acted as a consultant for Lewisham's New Opportunities Fund (NoF) ICT training for secondary music teachers, and is currently Co-ordinator of Greenwich Music Service.

ABOUT THE COMPOSER OF DJEMBÉ JAM AND DJEMBÉ FUNK

Tobias Stürmer is a percussionist, drummer, multi-instrumentalist, producer and composer. He is a graduate of Mannes College of Music, New York and holds an MMus in Ethnomusicology from SOAS, University of London. He performs professionally on the London jazz, Latin and African music scenes as well as on the contemporary dance scene. He has produced his own CDs of jazz and experimental music and has also undertaken various recording projects in Uganda and Senegal.

ABOUT MUSIC EXPRESS YEAR 7

Music Express Year 7 provides teaching activities that are imaginative, inspiring and fun. It is user-friendly, well planned, fully resourced and based on good practice for teaching and learning. It promotes inclusion, draws upon a range of music from diverse cultures and enables all pupils to build on their already established skills and knowledge in a purposeful and engaging way.

Each book provides a unit of six weekly lessons, which are intended to be taught over a half term. Each lesson follows the same pattern: objectives are identified and shared with the pupils and the lesson then unfolds through clear activities delivered in a range of styles. The lessons are clearly set out into starter (focus), core activities and plenary, and each lesson provides a suggestion for appropriate homework.

Each lesson is designed to last 50 minutes and approximate timings are provided in the book for each activity.

Suggestions are provided in each lesson for activities which might be used as extension work for students or to extend the lesson for schools with more time available.

This resource offers:

- ways of using a keyboard for appropriate activities;
- ways to incorporate ICT into music teaching and learning;
- extension activities;
- printouts for pupils' files;
- instrumental parts where required;
- all music on CD;
- additional background information on the composers and pieces featured in the activities.

A key feature of the *Music Express Year 7* resource is the use of video clips in which composers and musicians demonstrate and explain their musical thinking. Pupils have the opportunity to reflect on and adopt their thought processes as models for their own learning.

USING MUSIC EXPRESS YEAR 7 AS A SCHEME OF WORK

Music Express Year 7 fulfils the requirements of the Music National Curriculum of England, of Wales and of Northern Ireland and supports the 5-14 National Guidelines for Scotland.

It is inspired and informed by units in the QCA Key Stage 3 scheme of work, but the programmes do not necessarily follow the units exactly. The QCA expectations and lesson objectives are embedded in the units which are designed to enable pupils to meet the standards expected of levels 4 and 5.

The series has been written and created to support high quality teaching and learning and to raise the standards of achievement in music at Key Stage 3. Lessons throughout the unit include reference to:

- the use of evidence and dialogue to identify where pupils are in their musical learning, where they need to go and how best to get there;
- the opportunity for pupils to identify what needs improving and how they can do so;
- peer and self assessment;
- analysis and evaluation of musicians in action to help develop the competence and confidence of every learner;
- clear indication of managing music lessons in a range of whole class, group and individual teaching and learning situations;
- ICT strategies.

Each unit has all the content required for each lesson leaving the teacher to focus on their teaching skills.

THE UNITS

There are six units in Music Express Year 7, published as six separate Book + CD + CD-ROM packs. Below is a list of the titles available in the series:

BOOK1: BRIDGING UNIT (LINKS TO QCA UNIT 1)

Bridging unit is a composing unit that builds on the vast range of musical experiences in Year 6 and is designed, therefore, to help address the wide range of skills, knowledge and understanding that pupils bring to Year 7.

Pupils work initially with simple rhythmic and melodic patterns and, following a workshop style, they use improvisation as a means to composition. Through a commissioned piece of music, pupils listen to and observe the composing process, and in a series of video clips showing an interview with the composer, they gain an insight into his creative thinking. Pupils complete a composition and are able to consider the strengths of their work against clearly described assessment criteria and set their own targets for future learning.

BOOK 2: PERFORMING TOGETHER (PROGRESSES FROM YEAR 5/6 UNIT 20)

This unit develops and demonstrates pupils' ability to prepare and take part in a large group performance. It provides an opportunity for pupils to maintain and develop the invaluable skills of learning by ear, reading simple notation, rehearsing a part and working as an ensemble. All parts are available on the CD and CD-ROM. Principles of preparation unfold throughout the unit and the flexibility of the material provided (eg opportunities for two-part singing, solo spots, improvisation and simple movement/dance routines) ensures that everyone can be included.

The unit is an important foundation for work in arranging and song writing later in the year. It also provides a useful basis for those pupils wanting to start a band or group out of school, who will need to learn how to rehearse and perform the songs they want to play.

BOOK 3: MUSICAL CYCLES (WEST AFRICA) (LINKS TO QCA UNIT 4)

Musical cycles (West Africa) combines performing, listening and composition activities to explore the structures and key characteristics of West African music and its instruments. Teaching and learning are illustrated through video clips and clearly described workshop activities that explore musical cycles, signals and rhythmic and melodic improvisation. Listening is integral to the work and CD extracts include a traditional rhythm from Guinea/Sierra Leone, and recordings of performances by Mamady Keïta and the Malian singer, Oumou Sangaré. The unit unfolds to enable pupils either to complete a composition activity, modelled by a professional composer, or to prepare a performance of *Djolé*.

BOOK 4: MUSICAL STRUCTURES (LINKS TO QCA UNIT 2)

This unit is based on the QCA unit covering musical structures. Pupils learn about the principles of repetition and contrast that underpin ternary and rondo forms in Western European music.

The unit guides pupils practically through key features of musical structures, including phrases, cadence, chord structure, chord progression and major and minor tonalities, using as illustration some of the great examples of the styles and genres.

BOOK 5: ARRANGING MUSIC (LINKS TO QCA UNIT 6)

Building on the *Performing together* unit *(Music Express Year 7 Book 2)* pupils learn about arranging techniques through listening to and performing different arrangements of a traditional spiritual and an original spiritual-style composition.

Pupils develop critical judgements on the characteristics of each arrangement by exploring the historical and social context of the spiritual as a genre. They learn about the tools of the arranger, revisiting chords and encountering scales, counter-melodies, and instrumentation, which they then use to create their own arrangements.

BOOK 6: MUSICAL CLICHÉS (LINKS TO QCA UNIT 5)

Musical clichés is the last of the six units – the finale to the *Music Express Year 7* series. The unit develops pupils' ability to recognise, analyse and use a range of musical conventions used in a specific musical genre.

They listen to and analyse a variety of pieces of music and are asked to identify characteristics used in blockbuster movie trailers, conventions used by composers and their instrumental techniques, some of which have become clichés through frequent use. They then improvise, compose and perform their own piece of music using and developing these conventions.

Please note – we have not included a separate Soundscapes (ICT) unit: instead we have integrated ICT into each unit by offering the opportunity to develop objectives through ICT, electronic keyboards and/or classroom instruments and acoustic instruments.

PREPARATION AND PLANNING

Music Express Year 7 Book 3 is designed to minimise preparation time.

Learning objectives and outcomes are given at the start of each lesson. **Teaching tips** also provide differentiation and assessment, and there is an exemplar lesson plan on the CD-ROM.

The unit and lesson aims are provided on the CD-ROM both in a **Presentation** and on printouts for the teacher to view with the pupils. The assessment criteria are also provided as a printout on the CD-ROM.

A complete list of resources is given at the start of each lesson. Key words are highlighted in bold in the activity text when they are first introduced and their definitions are given on each page under **Key words.** There is a glossary at the back of the book and a printout of key words is also provided for pupils on the CD-ROM.

Icons next to the activity headings indicate what you will need to prepare:

Printouts icon: some activities require worksheets or background information to be printed out from the CD-ROM.

Optional printouts icon: for some activities worksheets are suggested but are not essential to the activity.

CD icon: details which audio tracks are required.

Video clips icon: you will need to have a computer and data projector set up to show the video clips. Video clips 1–11 are 2–3 minutes long. Video clips A–Q are 10–30 seconds long.

Teachers' reference video clip icon: we suggest you watch the video clip before the lesson as preparation.

Audacity files icon: you will need to have a computer (with Audacity installed from the CD-ROM) and data projector or whiteboard set up.

Picture gallery: you can either view these on a whiteboard or download printable versions to use in a classroom display or to provide as handouts.

Presentation: you will need to have a computer and data projector or whiteboard set up to show the unit overview and learning intentions for each lesson in a presentation on the CD-ROM.

Other resources required are listed under **Resources** in the book at the start of each lesson.

CLASSROOM MANAGEMENT AND WORKING WITH WEST AFRICAN MUSIC

Music Express Year 7 is designed to enhance and support individual teaching styles. It is not intended to dictate paradigms or pedagogy but rather to make suggestions. Each lesson includes suggestions for managing the activities, including ideas for whole class teaching, small group teaching and giving opportunities to individuals to show leadership and to work on their own. How the activities are managed may need to be adapted to meet the physical environments and cultures of individual schools. Lessons towards the end of each unit expect pupils to demonstrate more independence in the personal management of their learning as the questions and tasks become generally more open.

Like all units in the series, *Musical Cycles (West Africa)* is rich in extension activities, teaching tips and background information, which will help teachers place pupils' learning in context. There are alternative keyboard activities and ICT activities for every lesson, catering for a range of classroom situations. However, it should be noted that pupils will gain the best appreciation of West African music from being able to use and experiment with live acoustic instruments.

You will find it helpful to consider the following when teaching this unit:

Music in West Africa is learnt by ear, often over long periods of time. Whilst this teaching technique cannot be replicated in the classroom, it provides us with the opportunity to focus on active listening skills. Regular reinforcement of new material is essential in this learning process and *Musical Cycles (West Africa)* has been structured to allow pupils to re-visit rhythms throughout the unit. Notation is provided as a helpful short-cut when time is limited but learning by ear will be the most effective way for pupils to internalise rhythms in the long-term.

West African music demands the active participation of performers and audiences. It is vital that musicians are able to communicate and respond to each other whilst playing, as the music is not written down. The activities in *Musical Cycles (West Africa)* provide teachers with the opportunity to encourage participation, awareness of fellow performers, awareness of the audience and the ability to listen actively.

ELECTRONIC KEYBOARDS

Many schools are equipped with electronic keyboards and many pupils will relish the idea of learning to play the keyboard. The keyboard's functions can easily be taught and exploited to achieve musical learning objectives. Laying down the foundations of good technique is an important aspect of Year 7 keyboard work. In *Music Express Year 7* keyboard tuition starts from the very beginning, providing materials to demonstrate good hand positions, emphasising the importance of developing both hands in playing and establishing an understanding of fingering.

One keyboard per pupil is the ideal situation, but if pupils are sharing, ensure that partners swap places regularly.

Each unit provides activities both for the beginner and more confident player, but teachers must remember that each unit has higher expectations of achievement and any pupils who miss the earlier units may miss some important developmental work.

Fingering is suggested throughout the unit, but it can be changed, or at times ignored if it becomes too much of an impediment to the creative process.

It is not practical to discuss here the many brands and models of keyboard available in such a fast developing market. However, *Music Express Year 7* does assume that the keyboards which schools use will support some basic functions: eg timbre, tempo, style and volume. The facility to record will also be invaluable.

Please note that teaching activity time does not include familiarising yourself with keyboard functionality and ICT software and, depending on experience, you might need to allow extra planning time to do this.

ICT

Many of the activities in *Music Express Year 7* will benefit from the use of a computer and whiteboard to display the supporting materials found on the CD-ROM.

In addition, some activities have specific ICT activities, details of which can be found at the end of each lesson.

Some of the ICT activities are led by the teacher from the front of the class using a whiteboard, for example, using a karaoke player in Book 2. For these activities make sure that the computer's sound output is connected to a classroom hi-fi (or equivalent), so that pupils can hear clearly while they clap rhythms or sing.

Some of the ICT activities require pupils to work independently in groups, for example using a midi sequencer in Book 1. This might make it necessary for the group using the computer to use headphones, if, for example, the rest of the class is working in groups with their instruments in the same area. Some music departments will have more than one computer, in which case teachers may be able to involve more groups in the ICT activities.

All the ICT activities should be deliverable on either a PC or a Mac computer. Software guidance is given on the CD-ROM.

SINGING

Music Express Year 7 does not provide instruction on using the voice – however, warm-up exercises and guidance are provided. Do remind pupils to put as little pressure on the throat as possible and instead support the sound with air from the diaphragm. Often pupils sing from the throat – forcing the air in this way can easily lead to cracked notes or neck strain, particularly in the adolescent voice. Singing from the diaphragm should create a warm, rich sound with extensive dynamic possibilities.

It is a common mistake to put less effort into singing quietly. Remind singers to use more air and greater effort to support a quiet note. In this way they will be able to make a quiet note that is both potent and sustained.

Some pupils will find it hard to pitch a note accurately. *Music Express Year 7* frequently uses a call and response format, as it gives pupils less time to worry. Being able to hear a tune in their heads first will help pupils to vocalise the internal sound correctly.

A warm-up is a useful and important activity to avoid strained voices and to get pupils in the right frame of mind for singing. An effective activity is to use the letter 'F' sound. Take a deep breath and start the sound slowly, gradually quickening, like a steam engine pulling away from the platform. Encourage the pupils to feel the push from their diaphragm and to watch and feel their own stomachs going in and out.

ASSESSMENT

Music Express Year 7 has several layers of assessment. As an initial support, Teaching tips are provided throughout each lesson. These give further clarification of aspects of the lesson and points that might be of particular benefit to the new teacher. At the end of each lesson there is a summary of points for assessment. These, together with the plenary sessions, combine to provide an ongoing picture of whole class development. They provide an opportunity for the pupils and the teacher to decide what stage the pupils are at in their learning, where they need to go and how best to get there. Major pieces of work towards the end of each unit have an assessment sheet supporting the National Curriculum level descriptions and an opportunity for self, peer and teacher assessment to consider the quality of the work. These build to give a profile of progress for each pupil. Each unit includes an end of unit evaluation that pupils have the opportunity to complete.

MUSICAL CYCLES (WEST AFRICA): OUTLINE

Lesson 1 Rhythmic skills

OBJECTIVES

By the end of the lesson pupils should:

- know about cyclic patterns and pulse;
- have started to learn the dunun cyclic patterns for *Djolé*.

OUTCOMES

Pupils:

- copy rhythm patterns accurately;
- invent four-beat rhythm patterns;
- create their own cyclic rhythm patterns;
- learn a set of traditional dunun cyclic patterns.

Lesson 2 Signals and polyrhythms

OBJECTIVES

By the end of the lesson pupils should:

- learn about musical signals;
- consolidate their understanding of cyclic patterns;
- learn the djembé parts for *Djolé*.

OUTCOMES

Pupils:

- give and respond to musical signals;
- play a range of cyclic patterns using voices, body percussion and drums;
- begin to improvise eight-beat rhythmic phrases.

Lesson 3 Melody and song

OBJECTIVES

By the end of the lesson pupils should:

- learn about melodic improvisation in a West African piece of music.

OUTCOMES

Pupils:

- improvise short melodic phrases;
- sing and play within a call and response structure;
- identify a range of instruments through listening.

Lesson 4 Starting to compose

OBJECTIVES

By the end of the lesson pupils should:

- develop an understanding of composing within a given framework inspired by traditional West African structures;
- begin to explore ways of notating and evaluating their work.

OUTCOMES

Pupils:

- compose a rhythm piece within a given composition framework using structures such as signals and cyclic patterns;
- represent their ideas through graphic and/or rhythm grid notation;
- use self and peer evaluation to assess their work in progress.

Lesson 5 Developing and rehearsing

OBJECTIVES

By the end of the lesson pupils should:

- have improved and developed their composition or performance;
- have begun to plan the way in which they wish their music to be performed;
- continue to notate and begin to record their work.

OUTCOMES

Pupils:

- represent their ideas through graphic and/or rhythm grid notation;
- work as a group to evaluate their composition so far.

Lesson 6 Bringing it all together

OBJECTIVES

By the end of the lesson pupils should:

- be able to perform *Djolé* or their own composition to the rest of the class;
- be able to appraise their own work and the work of other groups.

OUTCOMES

Pupils:

- perform *Djolé* or their own composition to the class;
- identify and evaluate the musical ideas within their own work and the work of others and how they fit together;
- evaluate their work.

Lesson 1 Rhythmic skills

Focus

1	Copying rhythm patterns	>> ICT
2	Build up cyclic rhythm patterns and combine to create polyrhythms	>> ICT
3	Watch an extract of a performance of *Djolé*	
4	Learn the dunun and bell cyclic patterns for *Djolé*	>> KEYBOARD >> ICT

Plenary

Lesson 2 Signals and polyrhythms

Focus

1	Revise the dunun and bell cyclic patterns for *Djolé*	>> KEYBOARD >> ICT
2	Learn to play and respond to a signal	
3	Learn the djembé cyclic patterns for *Djolé*	>> KEYBOARD >> ICT
4	Begin to improvise rhythms	>> KEYBOARD >> ICT

Plenary

Lesson 3 Melody and song

Focus

1	Learn the call and response song *Laïlaïko*	>> KEYBOARD >> ICT
2	Exploring call and response rhythms	>> KEYBOARD
3	Listen to *Kayi ni wura* to explore melodic call and response	
4	Melodic improvisation	>> KEYBOARD >> ICT

Plenary

Lesson 4 Starting to compose

Focus

1	Pupils are introduced to their composition or performance task	
2	Pupils develop and practise the main rhythm section for their piece	>> KEYBOARD >> ICT
3	Pupils watch a video clip which provides ideas for building a structure	>> KEYBOARD >> ICT

Plenary

Lesson 5 Developing and rehearsing

Focus

1	Pupils share ideas and decide a structure for their composition or performance	>> KEYBOARD >> ICT
2	Pupils consider ways to reorchestrate their rhythm piece	>> ICT
3	Pupils refine and rehearse their composition or version of *Djolé*	>> KEYBOARD >> ICT

Plenary

Lesson 6 Bringing it all together

Focus

1	Pupils rehearse their composition or version of *Djolé* in their groups	>> KEYBOARD >> ICT
2	Pupils perform their composition or version of *Djolé*	>> ICT
3	Evaluate and assess the performances	>> KEYBOARD >> ICT

Plenary

OBJECTIVES

By the end of the lesson pupils should:

- know about cyclic patterns and pulse;
- have started to learn the dunun cyclic patterns for *Djolé*.

OUTCOMES

Pupils:

- copy rhythm patterns accurately;
- invent four-beat rhythm patterns;
- create their own cyclic rhythm patterns;
- learn a set of traditional dunun cyclic patterns.

RESOURCES

AUDIO CD
Tracks 1–10

CD-ROM
- Presentation
- Printouts 1–7
- Video clips 1–5
- Picture gallery
- Teacher information (optional)

INSTRUMENTS
- Claves or other available hand-held percussion
- Electronic keyboards (optional)

ICT
- Whiteboard or computer and data projector with sound
- Audacity installed (optional); wav files

PREPARATION
- Before the lesson, watch video clip 2 which demonstrates using body percussion and vocalisation to teach rhythms.
- Learn the cyclic pattern for activity 2 and the dunun and bell cyclic patterns for activity 4 before the lesson.

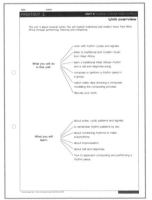

Printout 1: Unit overview

Focus — 10 mins — 🎥 1 — ⑴ ⑵ ⑶ ⑷ — ▢ **Presentation**

- Introduce the learning intentions for this unit using the presentation on the CD-ROM or printout 1.

- Introduce the pupils to West Africa and its music by:
  - discussing which countries are in West Africa, using **Maps of West Africa** (printout 2);
  - discussing which instruments are from West Africa, and displaying the pictures in the picture gallery on the CD-ROM;
    (eg dununs, djembés, talking drums, kpanlogo and sabar drums, shakers, bells);
  - asking pupils about their existing knowledge or impressions of West African music or Africa in general.

- All watch video clip 1 which shows aspects of everyday life and music in Senegal. (See **Notes to accompany video clip 1**, printout 3, for more information.)

- Discuss the learning intentions for this lesson using the presentation on the CD-ROM or printout 4.

TEACHING TIP
Be aware that each country in West Africa has within it a variety of ethnic groups, each with its own language, customs and musical traditions, leading to a great variety of traditions within and across political borders.

1 Copying rhythm patterns

ICT page 17

10 mins — ⦿ 1–3 — 🎥 2

- Before the lesson watch video clip 2, which demonstrates how to use body percussion and vocalisation to teach rhythms effectively. (It includes examples of four- and eight-beat phrases.)

TEACHING TIP
Vocalisation is important when learning West African music by ear. Use any vocal sounds that you are comfortable with; they don't have to be those on the video clip. Make sure your voice communicates the pitch of the sound, eg *boom* for bass and *pe* or *de* for higher notes.

- Group the class in a circle to ensure good eye contact and full participation. If possible get everyone on their feet with enough room to move safely.

- Explain the term **pulse**, then ask an able pupil to keep an audible steady pulse using claves, or other available hand-held percussion.
  (If you prefer to keep time yourself, wear a set of ankle bells and tap your foot to provide an audible regular pulse while keeping your hands free.)

- Count four steady beats out loud to start, then clap or vocalise a simple rhythm over four beats for the class to copy on the next four beats (or use CD tracks 1–2), eg

- After the pattern has been copied correctly, change to a different pattern and gradually introduce more syncopated patterns. Explain the term **syncopation**.

- Invite a confident pupil to take the lead. As the class becomes more confident, pass the lead around several different pupils.

- Next extend the phrase to eight beats (or use track 3). Count eight steady beats out loud to start.

TEACHING TIPS

Tracks 1–3 provide rhythms for the pupils to copy. Each rhythm is played twice: track 1 provides simple four-beat rhythms using claps and stamps only; track 2 provides more challenging rhythms and includes vocalisation, stamps, claps and finger clicks; track 3 provides eight-beat phrases consisting of claps and stamps using syncopated patterns that are West African in style.

Observe how each pupil copes with copying and remembering the pattern. Watch for those who can feel the steady pulse in their bodies.

2 Build up cyclic rhythm patterns and combine to create polyrhythms

⚙ ICT page 18

10 mins 🎥 3

- Before the lesson watch video clip 3, which demonstrates the cyclic pattern for this activity.

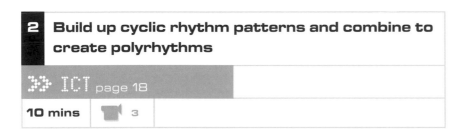

- Ask the class what the word 'cycle' means and to think of examples of cycles. *(Establish that a cycle refers to something that is circular or round and think about water cycle, life cycle, recycle, bicycle etc.)*

- Group the class in a circle (preferably standing up) and set an audible pulse as in activity 1.

- Count eight steady beats out loud and ask the class to copy, counting out loud immediately after you.

KEY WORDS

pulse – a steady beat.

syncopation – instead of accenting the strong beats (eg 1 2 3 4), syncopated music accents the weak beats – the off-beats (eg 1 2 3 4 or 1 + 2 + 3 + 4 +).

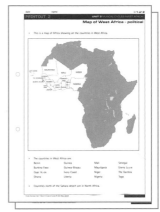

Printout 2: Maps of West Africa (2 pages)

Printout 3: Notes to accompany video clip 1

Printout 4: Learning intentions lessons 1–6

■ Add each of the body percussion sounds in turn (as demonstrated in video clip 3 and shown on the previous page). Each time you add a sound, ask the class to copy you and only add the next sound once the class is confident.

■ Repeat continuously at a steady tempo so that the rhythm forms a cyclic pattern. Explain what is meant by the term **cyclic pattern**.

■ Ask the class to work in pairs for two minutes to create their own eight-beat rhythm to perform as a cyclic pattern using body percussion and voices. Encourage pupils to be creative with their rhythm, and make sure it has at least one silent beat (as shown in the second example in video clip 3).

TEACHING TIP

Encourage more able pupils to include syncopation in their rhythm, and explore interesting body percussion, eg clapping hands together with their partner. Pupils should avoid large movements, such as jumps, however, as they can make rhythmic accuracy more difficult.

■ Invite pairs to demonstrate their cyclic pattern to the rest of the class. Provide a steady audible pulse throughout.

■ Choose two cyclic patterns with contrasting rhythms for the rest of the class to learn. Half the class should perform one cyclic pattern; the other half should perform the other. Perform the two patterns separately and then together.

■ Listen to the effect created by playing the cyclic patterns together. Pupils should be able to hear how a third pattern emerges from the combination of the two cycles. Explain that this is called a **polyrhythm**.

EXTENSION ACTIVITY

The class performs the cyclic pattern shown on page 13 using body percussion, and as they do, you call out a body percussion sound for them to leave out for one repetition of the cyclic pattern, eg 'Leave out the stamps'. The class then performs the cyclic pattern without performing the stamps on beats 1 and 2 for one repetition.

(Call out instructions in good time. A good tip is to call the action you want left out next time as it is currently being played.)

3	Watch an extract of a performance of Djolé
5 mins	🎥 4

■ All watch an extract of *Djolé* (video clip 4). Explain that *Djolé* (pronounced jo-lay) is a traditional, celebration rhythm that originated with the Teminé people from the forest region of Guinea and Sierra Leone, but is now a popular rhythm played in many different versions throughout West Africa.

■ Encourage pupils to tap the pulse as they listen; then discuss the mood of the piece *(energetic, joyful, celebratory, etc)*.

■ Watch the video clip again, and explain that each instrument in the ensemble has a job to do. Discuss the instruments shown, eg:

• the cowbell and shaker are keeping the pulse;
• the three drums at the back are known as **dunun** drums; they are bass drums, each with a bell, and their role is to provide support for the music;
• the drums at the front are **djembés**; three are repeating cyclic patterns to add texture to the music; the leading djembé directs the rest of the group by giving signals and adds energy to the music through improvisation.

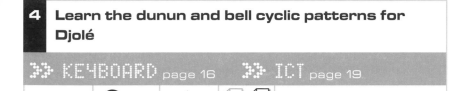

4 | **Learn the dunun and bell cyclic patterns for Djolé**

>> KEYBOARD page 16   **>> ICT** page 19

10 mins | ● 4-9 | 🎥 5 | 5 | 6

- Before the lesson learn the dunun and bell rhythms for *Djolé* yourself using printout 5 or page 52, tracks 4–9 and video clip 5 so that you are able to teach the pupils with confidence. (You will need to decide whether the full or simplified versions are suitable for the different abilities within your class.)

- Display *Background information: dunun drums* (printout 6) to show the three bass drums: **dununba** (largest), **sangban** (mid-sized) and **kenkeni** (smallest). Explain that collectively these drums are called dunun drums.

- Explain that pupils are going to learn the three dunun and bell cyclic patterns for *Djolé*. Teach each of the rhythms in turn using voices and body percussion only:
  - explain that they are going to tap their right thigh for the drum and their left thigh for the bell;
  - set up a clear, audible pulse as described in activity 1 or, if necessary, use tracks 4–6 or 7–9 which provide each part for the class to copy (tracks 4–6 are the full rhythms; 7–9 are the simplified rhythms);
  - demonstrate the dununba rhythm four times to the class tapping it on thighs and vocalising the sound (demonstrated in video clip 5). The pupils copy the rhythm immediately after you;
  - practise repeating the rhythm as a cyclic pattern until it is secure;
  - repeat the process with the sangban and then the kenkeni rhythms.

- Divide the class into three equal groups. Start the first group with the dununba cyclic pattern; once it is secure, add the second group with the sangban pattern; once they are secure, add the third group with the kenkeni pattern.

TEACHING TIPS

When teaching music by ear it is important to maintain good eye contact with pupils and to keep a steady, audible pulse going at all times. If pupils are having difficulty feeling the pulse, you may like to encourage them to walk on the spot in time with it.

Depending on pupils' ability and confidence, it may be necessary to only learn two rhythms to begin with. In this case, teach the dununba and sangban rhythms and play the kenkeni rhythm yourself using a cowbell or another loud hand-held percussion instrument.

To help pupils hear how the different rhythms fit together, try to sing one rhythm yourself while the class rehearses another. You may also like to show the pupils video clip 5.

Plenary

5 mins | ● 10

- All listen to track 10 – an excerpt of *Djolé* as played by master drummer Mamady Keïta and his troupe Sewa Kan. Discuss how this recording is different from the extract in video clip 4.
  (eg it is faster and includes singing.)

- Revise what is meant by the terms cyclic pattern, syncopation and polyrhythm.

KEY WORDS

cyclic pattern – a musical pattern that repeats continuously.

polyrhythm – more than one rhythm played at the same time.

dunun – a Mandinka bass drum often played in a set of three different sizes, each with a bell, to accompany the djembé.

djembé – a solo or lead drum made from a single piece of wood shaped like a goblet with a playing head made from goat skin.

dununba – largest dunun.

sangban – mid-sized dunun.

kenkeni – smallest dunun.

Printout 5: Rhythm grid for Djolé dunun cyclic patterns

Printout 6: Background information: dunun drums

ASSESSMENT FOR LEARNING

Who can feel the length of the phrases?

Who can copy rhythm patterns accurately?

Who is able to master physical coordination of body percussion cyclic patterns?

Who is confident creating their own cyclic patterns?

Printout 7: West African popular musicians

Homework 7

■ Pupils find out about West African popular music by researching one or more of the following musicians:

· Oumou Sangaré (from Mali);

· Fela Kuti (from Nigeria);

· Youssou N'Dour (from Senegal).

They fill in the information on *West African popular musicians* (printout 7).

KEYBOARD   (see page 15)

4   Learn the dunun and bell cyclic patterns for Djolé

10 mins   ● 4-9   🎥 4   🎥 5   📄 5   📄 6

■ Before the lesson learn the dunun and bell rhythms for *Djolé* yourself using printout 5 or page 52, tracks 4-9 and video clip 5, so that you are able to teach the pupils with confidence. (You will need to decide whether the full or simplified versions are suitable for the different abilities within your class.)

■ Display *Background information: dunun drums* (printout 6) to show the three bass drums: **dununba** (largest), **sangban** (mid-sized) and **kenkeni** (smallest). Explain that collectively these drums are called dunun drums.

■ Learn each of the three dunun and bell cyclic patterns in turn and then together, using only voices and body percussion, as described on page 15.

■ Listen again to the ensemble playing in video clip 4 (or use tracks 4–6 or 7–9 in which each dunun and bell rhythm is performed individually) and ask the class to describe the characteristic sounds of the three dunun.
(eg resonant, rounded, low, brittle etc)

■ On a keyboard, demonstrate how to select VOICE and then DRUM KIT, and show how each key corresponds to a different percussion sound. Choose three drum sounds and a bell sound with the class that approximate the dunun and bell heard in the recording (eg soft bass drums, mid toms or congas with agogo bells). Play each dunun and bell cyclic pattern to the class using those keys.

■ Pupils work in pairs at a keyboard to choose their own drum kit sounds for the three dunun and bell cyclic patterns. They practise each cyclic pattern in turn. Encourage them to record one into their keyboard memory and play the other two live with their recording.

■ Discuss with the class:

· how well the keyboard sounds matched the acoustic instrument sounds;

· how the pupils feel about recreating the *Djolé* rhythms using electronic keyboards.

RETURN TO PLENARY   (page 15)

ICT   (see page 12)

1 Copying rhythm patterns

10 mins

- You will need Audacity installed on your classroom computer, the display projected onto a screen or whiteboard and the sound output of the computer enabled. (See *Using Audacity* in the Teacher information section of the CD-ROM for further information.)

- Before the lesson watch video clip 2 for a demonstration of how to use body percussion and vocalisation to teach rhythms effectively. Group the class in a circle to ensure good eye contact and full participation, and ask the class to copy some four-beat rhythms as described on page 13.

- Import the file *4beat1.wav* from the CD-ROM into Audacity. If necessary, use the ZOOM buttons to make the rhythms clearly visible as they play:

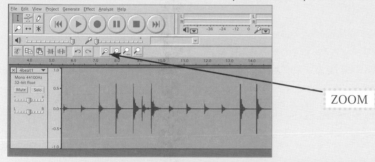

ZOOM

Press PLAY, and explain that this is an audio recording of somebody playing rhythms for them to copy. The waveform display shows the sound vibrations made as the rhythms were recorded. The hand claps, stamps and pulse are clearly visible, and the moving song position line passes each sound as it plays.

- Discuss whether anyone has seen similar waveform displays in other software they may have used *(eg Ejay, Cubase, Logic, Acid, Fruity Loops, Reason)*.

- Play the file again, and ask the class to copy each rhythm in the gap provided, in time with the pulse. (Import *4beat2.wav* for more challenging rhythms, and *8beat.wav* for eight-beat rhythms.)

TEACHING TIPS

You can start playing from anywhere in the waveform, simply click on the waveform where you want to start and click on PLAY.

If pupils find one particular rhythm difficult, select and then loop play until they have mastered it. (See *Using Audacity* in the Teacher information section of the CD-ROM for information about selecting and looping.)

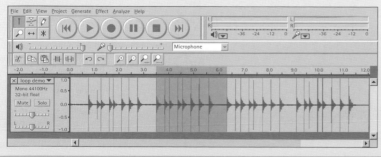

RETURN TO ACTIVITY 2   (page 13)

ICT   (see page 13)

2 | **Build up cyclic rhythm patterns and combine to create polyrhythms**

10 mins | 🎥 3 | 📁 AUDACITY |

- Before the lesson watch video clip 3, which demonstrates the cyclic pattern for this activity.

- Ask the class what the word 'cycle' means and to think of examples of cycles. *(Establish that a cycle refers to something that is circular or round and think about water cycle, life cycle, recycle, bicycle etc.)*

- Import *pulse.wav* from the CD-ROM into Audacity. Play the file and explain that it is an audio recording of somebody playing a pulse on a pair of ankle bells.

- Demonstrate how to loop the pulse (see *Using Audacity* in the Teacher information section of the CD-ROM), and use the looped recording of the pulse to provide a steady beat as the class learns the cyclic rhythm pattern, as described on pages 13–14.

TEACHING TIP

To loop play a whole file, select all (control key + A on a PC, or apple key + A on a Mac), then hold down shift as you either press the spacebar or click on the PLAY button.

- Explain what is meant by the term **cyclic pattern**, and explain that ICT is good at repeating short phrases to make cyclic patterns or 'loops', and that drum loops in dance music are like cyclic patterns in West African music.

- Import *dunfull.wav* and *sanfull.wav*, and loop play the files. As the rhythm loops, mute each track to demonstrate how they sound individually, then play both together to demonstrate the combined effect. Explain that this is called a **polyrhythm**. Tell the class they will be learning to play these rhythms.

◀◀ RETURN TO ACTIVITY 3   (page 14)

ICT   (see page 15)

4   Learn the dunun and bell cyclic patterns for Djolé

10 mins   4–9   5   5   6   AUDACITY

- Before the lesson learn the dunun and bell rhythms for *Djolé* yourself using printout 5 or page 52, tracks 4–9 and video clip 5, so that you are able to teach the pupils with confidence. (You will need to decide whether the full or simplified versions are suitable for the different abilities within your class.)

- Display *Background information: dunun drums* (printout 6) to show the three bass drums: **dununba** (largest), **sangban** (mid-sized) and **kenkeni** (smallest). Explain that collectively these drums are called dunun drums.

- Import the three dunun and bell rhythms *dunfull.wav*, *sanfull.wav* and *kenfull.wav* into Audacity (or use the simplified versions depending on the different abilities within your class).

- Select four beats of rhythm so that each plays only once through. Loop play, and demonstrate how each rhythm sounds on its own, and then how they interact together by using the SOLO or MUTE buttons for each track. (You may find it easier to choose the second four beats of the rhythm and to set the loop to end just before the first beat of the pulse, as shown below.)

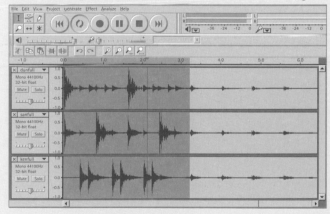

- Note that each rhythm is followed by a gap where only the pulse is heard. Solo each track in turn and loop play. Ask the class to listen carefully to the rhythm then copy in the gap provided. Ask pupils to tap their right thigh for the drum and their left thigh for the bell, and vocalise the sound as well (as demonstrated in video clip 5).

- When most of the class are confident performing the rhythms with the recording, divide the class into three equal groups and practise layering the three rhythms as cyclic patterns away from the computer.

TEACHING TIPS

If the class finds it hard to perform the three rhythms at the same time, use the computer to play one of the rhythms while the class performs the other two.

Please note that the *wav* files are eight beats long (rather than four) so that they will loop with the full version of the djembé 2 cyclic pattern (which is eight beats long) next lesson.

RETURN TO PLENARY   (page 15)

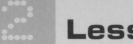

Lesson 2   Signals and polyrhythms

OBJECTIVES

By the end of the lesson pupils should:

- learn about musical signals;
- consolidate their understanding of cyclic patterns;
- learn the djembé parts for *Djolé*.

OUTCOMES

Pupils:

- give and respond to musical signals;
- play a range of cyclic patterns using voices, body percussion and drums;
- begin to improvise eight-beat rhythmic phrases.

RESOURCES

AUDIO CD
Tracks 10–29

CD-ROM
- Presentation
- Printouts 4–5, 8–9
- Video clips 4, 6, A–Q
- Teacher information (optional)

INSTRUMENTS
- Cowbell and shakers (or other available hand-held percussion)
- Variety of drums tuned to high, middle and low pitches (ideally a set of dunun drums and djembés)
- Beaters for dunun drums and bells
- Electronic keyboards (optional)

ICT
- Whiteboard or computer and data projector with sound
- Audacity installed (optional); wav files

PREPARATION
- Learn the djembé cyclic patterns for activity 3 before the lesson.

Printout 4: Learning intentions lessons 1–6

Focus		
5 mins	4	**Presentation**

- Invite pupils to talk briefly about the musician they researched for homework last lesson. You may wish to discuss one or more of the following points:

  • how many of the musicians used only traditional West African instruments and how many combined traditional and non-traditional instruments?

  • how was the music pupils listened to similar to music they listen to themselves?

  • what were the most common subjects for the musicians to sing about?

- Discuss the learning intentions for this lesson using the presentation on the CD-ROM or printout 4.

1 Revise the dunun and bell cyclic patterns for Djolé

>> KEYBOARD page 24   >> ICT page 26

5 mins	5	

- Ask the class if anyone can remember the three dunun and bell cyclic patterns for *Djolé* (dununba, sangban and kenkeni). Invite individuals to demonstrate each pattern using body percussion and vocalisation.

- Practise each pattern in turn by tapping it on thighs and vocalising, as described on page 15. (Refer to printout 5 or page 52, if necessary.)

- Divide the class into three equal groups and combine the cyclic patterns.

2 Learn to play and respond to a signal

10 mins	●	**11-21**	🎥	**A-K**

- Explain that traditional West African music is played without a conductor and is controlled by a **lead drummer**, or sometimes a **master drummer**. The lead (or master) drummer uses **signals** or **calls** to set the tempo, tell the other musicians when to start and stop playing and to tell any dancers when to change their movements.
(A signal is usually a short rhythmic phrase played by the lead or master djembé drummer.)

■ Listen to track 11 or watch video clip K to hear a traditional djembé signal that is used for many different pieces. Ask pupils to tap the pulse as they listen to the signal.

■ Learn the signal by copying it in the gaps provided on track 11, using voices or body percussion. When the pupils are confident doing this, transfer the signal to instruments.

■ Watch video clips A–E (for full rhythms) or F–J (for simplified rhythms) which shows how the dunun players respond to the signal to start and stop playing. Notice that the lead drummer plays one beat before starting the signal to announce that he is about to play the signal.

■ Use tracks 12–16 (full) or 17–21 (simplified) to practise performing the dunun cyclic patterns on body percussion in response to the signal. Make sure that:

• the dunun rhythms start firmly on the first beat following the signal;
• on hearing the end signal pupils complete the rhythm and all finish with one extra beat on the drum.

■ Once pupils are confident performing the three dunun and bell cyclic patterns on body percussion, move on to using percussion instruments. Either play or vocalise the signals yourself or invite a confident pupil to do this. Divide the rest of the class into three equal groups to play each of the cyclic patterns. (The pupil playing the signal may decide whether to start playing the signal to finish on the first beat of the cycle or announce it with an extra beat first.)

TEACHING TIPS

It is important that pupils have properly internalised the rhythms and can feel the way that they interconnect before they move on to using instruments.

If you do not have a set of dunun drums available, use any drums tuned to low, middle and high pitches (for example timpani, snare drum with snare removed, tambour) and play with a beater. Alternatively, junk percussion such as bins, buckets and tubs often work just as well, if not better.

Encourage pupils to say the rhythms out loud while they play them, as vocalisation is a key element in learning West African music by ear.

3 **Learn the djembé cyclic patterns for Djolé**

>> KEYBOARD page 24   **>> ICT** page 27

| 15 mins | ⏺ 22-27 | 🎥 4, 6, L-Q | 🗐 8 | 🗐 9 |

■ Before the lesson learn the two djembé rhythms for *Djolé* yourself, using printout 8 or page 53, tracks 22–27 and video clips L–Q. (You will again need to decide whether to use the full or simplified versions.)

TEACHING TIPS

The djembé rhythms provided have been adapted especially for whole class work with a range of drums and can be played using only bass and tone sounds if you wish.

Watch video clip 6 before the lesson to see how *Djolé* can be played using a range of classroom percussion and junk instruments. This may provide you with some ideas if you do not have djembés or a wide range of skinned percussion.

Please note: the signal used in the video clips of the performances of *Djolé* is a more complex call and response signal to the one introduced in activity 2 and will be discussed in the plenary for this lesson.

KEY WORDS

lead drummer – a drummer who directs the rest of the ensemble and any dancers by providing signals and solo improvisations.

master drummer – a drummer acknowledged by other musicians and members of the community to have complete technical mastery and a thorough understanding of the drum, its music and its culture.

signal – (sometimes referred to as a 'call') a musical phrase, usually a rhythm, that sets the tempo and indicates to other players when to start and stop playing.

Printout 5: Rhythm grid for Djolé dunun cyclic patterns

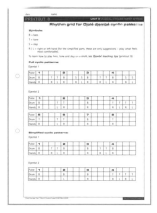

Printout 8: Rhythm grid for Djolé djembé cyclic patterns

Printout 9: Djembé teaching tips (2 pages)

■ Watch video clip 4 to revise the role of the djembés in the ensemble. *(One is the lead drummer, the others play cyclic patterns to add texture to the music).*

■ Explain that the pupils are now going to learn the djembé cyclic patterns. As with the dunun cyclic patterns, learn the rhythms vocally and using body percussion first before introducing instruments:

  • set up a clear, audible steady pulse;
  • demonstrate the first djembé rhythm (see printout 8) four times to the class using your right and left hands on your lap and vocalising the sounds. The pupils copy the rhythm four times immediately after you;
  • practise repeating the rhythm as a cyclic pattern until it is secure;
  • repeat this process with the second djembé rhythm.

■ Practise starting and stopping each cyclic pattern with the signal. Listen to tracks 22–23 or 25–26 to hear how the signal fits with each djembé rhythm or watch video clips L-Q. (Notice that the second full djembé cyclic pattern is an eight-beat phrase, so the signal to finish starts half way through it.)

■ Divide the class into two equal groups. Start the first group with the first djembé cyclic pattern and, once it is secure, add the second group with the second djembé cyclic pattern. (Listen to track 24 or 27 to hear both parts playing together in response to the signal.)

■ Once the class are confident using body percussion and voices to perform the rhythms, move on to using instruments. Explain that the djembé produces three different sounds: tone, slap and bass. If you are using djembés, go through ***Djembé teaching tips*** (printout 9) to learn how to produce the different sounds. (You may also like to watch video clips L-Q again.)

TEACHING TIP

Pupils can use other suitable drums, playing with a flat hand and closed fingers at the edge of the drum to achieve a tone sound and playing in the middle of the drum to achieve a bass sound.

EXTENSION ACTIVITY

Watch video clip 6 as a class to see and hear ***Djolé*** being played using a range of classroom percussion instruments. Ask pupils to identify which instruments are playing which part.

(The lead drummer is playing the bongos. The three dunun patterns are being played on an upturned box, a drum and a tulip block at the front of the group. The pulse is being played by claves and a cabasa. The two djembé patterns are being played on a woodblock, tambourine and cowbell in the middle at the back of the group.)

Listen again and identify the structure of the music. Each section is introduced by a signal.

Section 1		Section 2		Ending	
SIGNAL	Dunun and bell cyclic patterns and pulse.	SIGNAL	Dunun and bell cyclic patterns, pulse, djembé cyclic patterns and improvisation by the lead drummer.	SIGNAL	All play with the end of the signal.

4 Begin to improvise rhythms

>> KEYBOARD page 25   **>> ICT** page 27

10 mins ⦿ **28**

- Explain the term **improvisation**. Then invent a simple four-beat rhythmic phrase on a drum or using body percussion and, as a class, explore improvising a reply, eg

  - set a pulse, then invite a confident pupil to perform the four-beat phrase and demonstrate yourself improvising a four-beat reply, (it may help pupils unfamiliar with improvisation to ask them to try simple things to begin with, eg change only one part of the phrase or change the sound by vocalising it in a different way);
  - repeat the above, but invite a few pupils to improvise a four-beat reply;
  - demonstrate extending the reply to eight beats by repeating it or developing some of the ideas in it; then invite individuals to do the same;
  - if you have djembés available, explore developing the improvisation using a combination of tone, slap and bass sounds;
  - ask a group to perform the dunun and bell cyclic patterns and invite individuals to improvise a four- or eight-beat phrase over the top influenced by the feel of the accompaniment.

TEACHING TIP
Explore as many of the ideas above as suits the abilities and experience of your class.

- Listen to an excerpt of Mamady Keïta's performance of *Djolé* (track 28) to hear how the lead drummer is using different improvised solo passages to lift the music to its climax.

Plenary

5 mins ⦿ **10, 29**

- Listen to Mamady Keïta performing *Djolé* (track 10) and invite the class to tap the pulse.

- Explain that this recording uses a different signal to the one they have learnt. All listen to the signal on its own (track 29) and copy it in the gaps provided.

- Discuss whether pupils are finding it any easier:
  - to identify rhythm patterns in the music;
  - to remember rhythm patterns;
  - to keep a steady pulse.

Homework 5 8

- Hand out the grids for the dunun and djembé cyclic patterns for *Djolé* (printouts 5 and 8) and ask pupils to practise the patterns using body percussion, junk percussion or table tops.

improvisation – a performance created as it is played.

ASSESSMENT FOR LEARNING

Who is confident using their voices to vocalise rhythms?

Who engages with others when playing within an ensemble?

Who can perform well-maintained cyclic patterns with a steady pulse?

Who can give or follow clear signals?

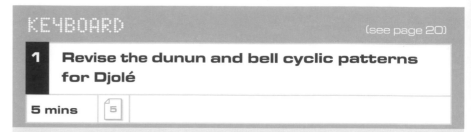

KEYBOARD (see page 20)

1 **Revise the dunun and bell cyclic patterns for Djolé**

5 mins ⌐5⌐

- Ask the class if anyone can remember the three dunun and bell cyclic patterns for *Djolé* (dununba, sangban and kenkeni). Invite individuals to demonstrate each pattern using body percussion and vocalisation.

- Practise each pattern in turn tapping the rhythm on thighs and vocalising, as described on page 15. (Refer to printout 5 or page 52, if necessary.)

- Once pupils are confident with the rhythms, they transfer them to the keyboard sounds they discovered last lesson. Suggest they set the metronome to 76 bpm (beats per minute) to practise the rhythms and, if possible, record all three cyclic patterns into the keyboard memory (sometimes called *user area* or *bank*) and listen carefully to check they play in time together.

TEACHING TIP
It is important that pupils make the physical act of using body percussion and vocalising the rhythms before moving on to the keyboard. Pulse and rhythm is physical and primarily 'felt'. The keyboard adds timbre and the facility to layer the three rhythms of *Djolé*.

RETURN TO ACTIVITY 2 (page 20)

KEYBOARD (see page 21)

3 **Learn the djembé cyclic patterns for Djolé**

15 mins ● 22-27 🎥 4, 6, L-Q ⌐8⌐

- Teach the pupils to perform the two djembé cyclic patterns for *Djolé* using body percussion as described on pages 21–22.

- Once pupils are confident with the rhythms, they work in pairs to transfer them to the drum kit sounds on their keyboard. They should choose three different sounds to represent tone, slap and bass and practise at 76 bpm.

- Once the rhythms are secure, pupils record them into two new tracks in the keyboard memory.

- They then practise starting and stopping each cyclic pattern with the signal. One person claps the signal and the other activates each of the cyclic patterns in turn. (Listen to tracks 22–27 to hear how the signal fits with each djembé rhythm or watch video clips L-Q.)

- If there is time (and particularly if your keyboards do not have the facility to record), ask pairs to join with other pairs at adjacent keyboards, or with pupils using acoustic percussion, to practise performing the dunun and djembé cyclic patterns together after a signal.

RETURN TO ACTIVITY 4 (page 23)

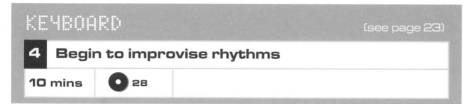

KEYBOARD   (see page 23)

4 **Begin to improvise rhythms**

10 mins   ● 28

■ Explain the term **improvisation**. Invent a simple four-beat rhythmic phrase using the drum kit sounds on the keyboard, and record it into your keyboard memory at a steady tempo. Explore improvising a reply to the phrase with the class, eg

- play the four-beat phrase and demonstrate improvising a four-beat reply;
- then invite a few pupils to improvise a four-beat reply (it may help pupils unfamiliar with improvisation to ask them to 'sort of copy' the first four-beat phrase by changing only one part of it);
- demonstrate extending the reply to eight beats by repeating it or developing some of the ideas in it; then invite individuals to do the same;
- explore developing the improvisation using a combination of three different drum sounds to represent tone, slap and bass;
- ask a group to perform the dunun and bell cyclic patterns, or use their recorded tracks, and invite individuals to improvise a four- or eight-beat phrase over the top influenced by the feel of the accompaniment.

TEACHING TIP
Explore as many of the ideas above as suits the abilities and experience of your class.

■ Listen to an excerpt of Mamady Keïta's performance of *Djolé* (track 28) to hear how the lead drummer is using different improvised solo passages to lift the music to its climax.

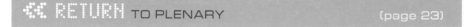

◄◄ RETURN TO PLENARY   (page 23)

ICT (see page 20)

1 Revise the dunun and bell cyclic patterns for Djolé

5 mins | 5 | AUDACITY

- Ask the class if anyone can remember the three dunun and bell cyclic patterns for *Djolé* (dununba, sangban and kenkeni). Invite individuals to demonstrate each pattern using body percussion and vocalisation.

- Import the three dunun *wav* files into Audacity. Listen to each rhythm once, then loop play and solo each track to remind pupils how each rhythm sounds as a cyclic pattern.

- Practise each rhythm in turn tapping the rhythm on thighs and vocalising, as described on page 15. (Refer to printout 5 or page 52 if necessary.)

- Solo the sangban track to provide a steady rhythmic accompaniment for the class to perform the dununba and kenkeni cyclic patterns to.

- Divide the class into three equal groups and combine the cyclic patterns.

EXTENSION ACTIVITY

Play *Switch* with the dunun cyclic patterns for *Djolé*:

- set the three rhythms to loop play, but mute the sangban and the kenkeni tracks so only the dununba can be heard;

- call 'switch' and quickly mute the dununba track and unmute the sangban track; the class perform the dununba cyclic pattern while listening to the sangban;

- when the class are ready, call 'switch' again, mute the sangban track and unmute the kenkeni track; the class performs the sangban cyclic pattern and listens to the kenkeni;

- continue switching between tracks, the class always perform the track they have just heard.

 RETURN TO ACTIVITY 2 (page 20)

ICT (see page 21)

3 **Learn the djembé cyclic patterns for Djolé**

15 mins ● 22-27 🎥 4, 6, L-Q 8 9 AUDACITY

■ Before the lesson learn the two djembé rhythms for *Djolé* yourself using printout 8 or page 53, tracks 22–27 and video clips L–Q.

■ Import the two djembé rhythms, *dje1full.wav* and *dje2full.wav*, into Audacity. (If the class learnt the simplified dunun rhythms, use the simplified djembé ones: *dje1simp.wav* and *dje2simp.wav*.)

■ Select the waveform area that represents the two rhythms (not the pulse). Loop play and demonstrate how each rhythm sounds on its own, and also how they interact together using the SOLO or MUTE button for each track.

■ Select all, so that the pulse section is now heard after each repetition. Solo and loop play the first djembé track and ask the class to:

  • listen carefully and tap the pulse quietly on their knees;
  • copy the rhythm using body percussion in the space provided (using right and left hands on laps as indicated on printout 8).

■ Repeat with the second djembé track.

■ When most of the class are confident copying the rhythms with the recording, ask them to perform each one continuously as a cyclic pattern without the computer.

■ Continue with the activities as described on page 22.

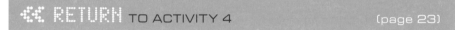
⋘ RETURN TO ACTIVITY 4 (page 23)

ICT (see page 23)

4 **Begin to improvise rhythms**

10 mins ● 28 AUDACITY

■ Revise the term **improvisation**. Then explore ways to improvise rhythms, as described on page 23, using *pulse.wav* in Audacity to provide the pulse.

■ As the class becomes more confident improvising over the pulse, invite a group to work at the computer with the three dunun files set to loop play and explore improvising a four- or eight-beat phrase over the top influenced by the feel of the accompaniment.

■ Listen to an excerpt of Mamady Keïta's performance of *Djolé* (track 28) to hear how the lead drummer is using different improvised solo passages to lift the music to its climax.

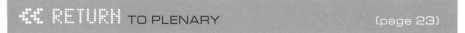
⋘ RETURN TO PLENARY (page 23)

Melody and song

OBJECTIVES

By the end of the lesson pupils should:

■ learn about melodic improvisation in a West African piece of music.

OUTCOMES

Pupils:

☐ improvise short melodic phrases;

☐ sing and play within a call and response structure;

☐ identify a range of instruments through listening.

RESOURCES

AUDIO CD
Tracks 30–35

CD-ROM
- Presentation
- Printouts 4–5, 8, 10–17
- Video clip 7
- Teacher information (optional)

INSTRUMENTS
- Bells and shakers (or other available hand-held percussion)
- Variety of drums tuned to high, middle and low pitches (ideally a set of dunun drums and djembés)
- Beaters for dunun drums and bells
- Tuned instruments
- Electronic keyboards (optional)

ICT
- Whiteboard or computer and data projector with sound
- Audacity installed (optional); wav files

Printout 4: Learning intentions lessons 1–6

Printout 5: Rhythm grid for Djolé dunun cyclic patterns

Focus

| **5 mins** | 4 | 5 | 8 | **Presentation** | |

■ Revise the dunun and djembé cyclic patterns for *Djolé* using body percussion or instruments (refer to printouts 5 and 8, if required), stopping and starting with the signal. If pupils remember the rhythms confidently, try the following:

- after a first signal the three dunun cyclic patterns start;
- after a second signal the two djembé cyclic patterns join in and a confident pupil improvises rhythmic ideas on a third djembé;
- after a third signal everyone finishes together.

■ Discuss the learning intentions for this lesson using the presentation on the CD-ROM or printout 4.

1 Learn the call and response song Laïlaïko

>> KEYBOARD page 31　　**>> ICT** page 33

| **10 mins** | ● 30-32 | 🎥 7 | 10 | 11 |

■ Explain the term **call and response** and ask pupils to name any examples of call and response songs (eg *Day Oh* from *Music Express Year 7 Book 1*).

■ Explain that call and response is an important feature of many songs from West Africa. Musicians use instruments or voices to ask musical questions and give musical replies.

■ Watch video clip 7: *Djolé performance.* Then introduce the song *Laïlaïko* using the background information on *Lyric sheet: Laïlaïko* (printout 10).

■ Teach the song to the class, starting with the responses. Use track 30 or set a steady audible pulse and sing the phrases yourself for the pupils to copy. (Display the lyrics on printout 10 or the melody on printout 11, if necessary, but it should be possible for the pupils to learn the responses by ear):

- start with the last phrase, 'Wawako, siko laïko', and repeat until the singing is clear and confident;
- next learn the two short, interrupting responses, 'Aïya!', making sure the pupils are comfortable with the syncopation;
- then you sing the calls (or use track 31) and ask the pupils to join in with the two responses in the correct places;
- repeat until the responses are prompt and confident.

TEACHING TIP

Pronunciation in West African songs may vary from region to region. Notice the difference in pronunciation of the word 'Laïlaïko' in the recording (lay-lay-ee-ko or lie-lie-ee-ko). The pronunciation guide on printouts 10 and 11 is based on the Mamady Keïta recording of *Djolé*.

■ All sing the whole song. You may like to invite a confident group of pupils to join you singing the call. (Sing along with track 31, if required.)

■ Invite a group of confident pupils to play the dunun cyclic patterns for *Djolé* to accompany the singing.

EXTENSION ACTIVITY

The phrase, 'Wawako, siko laïko', can be sung in harmony. Teach the class the harmony part on track 32 and combine this with singing the whole song all the way through.

2	**Exploring call and response rhythms**
KEYBOARD page 32	
10 mins ⊙ 33	

■ Explain that rhythms as well as melodies can follow a call and response structure. This is one of the structures that pupils may wish to use later in developing their own rhythmic compositions or performance pieces.

■ Clap this call and see if any pupils respond automatically with the response. (If none do, demonstrate the rhythm and explain that the first phrase is answered by the second.)

■ Listen to track 33, a simple rhythmic call and response. Ask pupils to join in clapping the response. (Note that the call starts just before the beat. The call is a longer phrase played by the djembé tones and slaps. The response consists of two djembé bass sounds.)

■ Ask pupils to work in pairs for a couple of minutes to devise their own call and response rhythms using voices, body percussion or instruments (if they are to hand). Both the call and the response should fit within eight beats of the pulse.

■ Invite pairs to demonstrate their call and response rhythms to the class.

EXTENSION ACTIVITY

Choose three different pairs whose call and response rhythms work well within eight beats. One by one, each pair should demonstrate their call and teach the rest of the class to join in with the matching response.

Practise performing each call and response pattern individually over eight beats as a cyclic pattern in time with an audible pulse. Then practise performing each call and response one after the other keeping time with the pulse.

The three pairs decide between themselves an order in which to play their calls, eg
    call 1 call 1 call 3 call 1 call 2 call 3 call 2 call 1
The pairs perform their calls and the class have to join in with the correct responses.

KEY WORDS

call and response – a type of song in which a soloist sings a phrase which is then responded to by a larger group of singers.

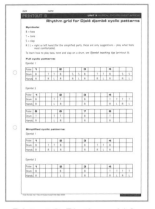

Printout 8: Rhythm grid for Djolé djembé cyclic patterns

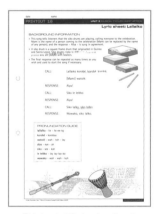

Printout 10: Lyric sheet: Laïlaïko

Printout 11: Laïlaïko melody

Printout 12: Background
information: Kayi ni wura

Printout 13: Kayi ni wura:
notation and suggestions

3 Listen to Kayi ni wura to explore melodic call and response

5 mins | 🔴 34 | 📄 12

- Listen to an excerpt from the song *Kayi ni wura* performed by Oumou Sangaré (track 34). Explain that the song is a homage to the spirits who guard the village, and means 'Evening greeting'. (Background information is provided on printout 12 on the CD-ROM.)

- Discuss the song with the class. Identify the instruments used, and listen for passages of unison singing, call and response singing, melodic improvisation and use of melodic cyclic patterns. Explain the term **unison**.
  (The instruments used are violin, shekere, kamalengoni, guitar, bass, djembé, backing chorus and lead vocalist. See printout 12 for more information.)

4 Melodic improvisation

KEYBOARD page 32   **ICT** page 33

15 mins | 🔴 35 | 📄 13

- Listen to an improvised passage played by the violin in *Kayi ni wura* (track 35). Explain that the violinist is improvising using notes of a pentatonic scale. Explain what is meant by the term **pentatonic scale**.

- Using voices or tuned instruments, practise singing or playing the opening and extended phrase of the violin solo using the notes A C D E and G, following the notation on printout 13, in time with an audible steady pulse.

A C D E G E   A C D E D D

TEACHING TIP
Please note that the tuning of the authentic instrument on the recordings will not match Western instruments precisely.

- Using this phrase as a starting point, pupils should work in pairs or small groups to improvise further pentatonic variations using the ideas suggested on printout 13. Encourage them to keep an audible steady pulse throughout.

- Invite pupils to share some of the melodic improvisations with the rest of the class. Play a steady pulse on a shaker and go around each pair or small group in turn.

Plenary

5 mins

- Discuss as a class:
  - what is improvisation?
  - what different skills does a player require to improvise?
    (eg a good sense of pulse, imagination, creativity etc.)
  - what are the characteristics of a successful improvisation?
    (eg it fits the character of the piece, it uses rhythmic or melodic ideas from the accompanying music, it adds excitement to the music etc.)

Homework 5 8 10 11 14 15

- Hand out the *Key words* (printout 14) for pupils to learn for homework.

- Encourage pupils to continue practising the dunun and djembé cyclic patterns for *Djolé* (using printouts 5 and 8, if required), and to practise singing or playing the song *Laïlaïko* using printouts 10, 11 or 15.

KEYBOARD   (see page 28)

1 Learn the call and response song Laïlaïko

10 mins ● 30-32 10 11 15

- Teach the call and response song, *Laïlaïko*, to the class as described on page 28.

- When the singing is clear and confident, pupils learn to play the song at the keyboard using printout 15.

- Explain that the song has been re-written so that it is easier to play on the keyboard. Demonstrate how to make the song play in tune with the recording by:
  - selecting TRANSPOSE on the keyboard;
  - holding down the written starting note, E, and at the same time pressing the minus key on the numeric keypad four times until -4 appears in the window. The E will now sound a C.

TEACHING TIPS

Please note that the tuning of the authentic instrument on the recordings will not match Western instruments precisely.

Advanced keyboard players may like to practise playing the song at pitch using printout 11.

- Divide the class into two groups to perform the song: one group plays or sings the calls and the other group the responses.

◀◀ RETURN TO ACTIVITY 2   (page 29)

KEY WORDS

unison – everyone playing or singing the same thing at the same time.

pentatonic scale – a five-note scale.

ASSESSMENT FOR LEARNING

Who can maintain their part in the rhythmic ensemble?

Who can identify elements in the listening excerpts?

Who volunteers improvisation ideas – rhythmic or melodic – in response to the given stimuli?

Printout 14: Key words
(2 pages)

Printout 15: Laïlaïko melody:
keyboard

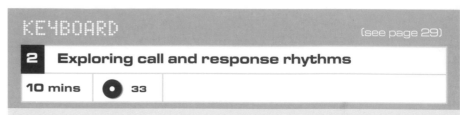

KEYBOARD (see page 29)

2 Exploring call and response rhythms

10 mins ● 33

- Explain that rhythms as well as melodies can also follow a call and response structure. This is one of the structures that pupils may wish to use later in developing their own rhythmic compositions or performance pieces.

- Demonstrate the two call and response rhythms, see page 29.

- Ask pupils to work in pairs for a couple of minutes at the keyboard, taking it in turns to improvise their own call and response rhythms using percussion voices from the drum kit sounds. Both the call and the response should fit within eight beats of a pulse. If needed, the metronome can be used to keep the pulse.

- Invite pairs to demonstrate their call and response rhythms to the class.

RETURN TO ACTIVITY 3 (page 30)

Printout 16: Kayi ni wura: notation and suggestions – keyboard (2 pages)

KEYBOARD (see page 30)

4 Melodic improvisation

15 mins ● 35 [16]

- Listen to an improvised passage played by the violin in *Kayi ni wura* (track 35). Explain that the violinist is improvising using notes of a pentatonic scale. Explain what is meant by the term **pentatonic scale**.

- Pupils learn to play the opening and extended phrase of the violin solo using the notes A C D E and G, following the notation on printout 16 in time with an audible steady pulse.

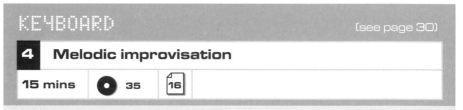

A C D E G E   A C D E D D

TEACHING TIP

Please note that the tuning of the authentic instrument on the recordings will not match Western instruments precisely.

- Using this phrase as a starting point, pupils work in pairs or small groups to improvise further pentatonic variations on the keyboard using the ideas suggested on printout 16. Encourage them to keep an audible steady pulse throughout.

- Invite pairs to share some of their melodic improvisations with the rest of the class.

RETURN TO PLENARY (page 31)

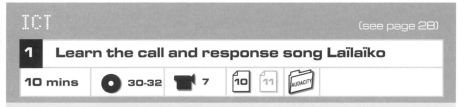

ICT (see page 28)

1 Learn the call and response song Laïlaïko

10 mins 30-32 7 10 11 AUDACITY

- Teach the call and response song, *Laïlaïko*, to the class as described on page 28, but use the three files: *lailaiko.wav*, *wawako.wav* and *aiya.wav* to help teach the different parts of the song as well as using your own voice. Using these files you can:

  · play the individual phrase you are teaching when you need to;
  · loop a phrase to hear it repeat in time;
  · provide a visual focus for the class as they listen;
  · let the computer lead the singing for a while to enable you to identify and support those who may need help.

- All sing the whole song. You may like to invite a confident group of pupils to join you in singing the call. (Sing along with track 31, if required.) Import the three dunun and two djembé files into Audacity and loop play to provide an accompaniment for the singing.

RETURN TO ACTIVITY 2 (page 29)

ICT (see page 30)

4 Melodic improvisation

15 mins 35 13 17 AUDACITY

- Listen to an improvised passage played by the violin in *Kayi ni wura* (track 35). Practise singing or playing the opening and extended phrase of the violin solo using the notes A C D E and G, following the notation on printout 13 in time with an audible steady pulse, as described on page 30.

- Using this phrase as a starting point, pupils work in pairs or small groups to improvise further pentatonic variations using the ideas suggested on printout 13. One or more groups may like to use ICT as a support for this activity. Suggest they:

  · import the three dunun and the two djembé files into Audacity;
  · solo the sangban track and set it to loop play to provide an audible steady pulse over which to improvise;
  · improvise over different combinations, or all, of the tracks once they are confident improvising over a steady pulse.

- Invite pupils to share some of their melodic improvisations with the rest of the class.

TEACHING TIP
Give pupils copies of *Pupils' guide to using Audacity* (printout 17) to work with, if required.

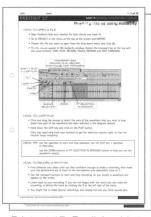

Printout 17: Pupils' guide to using Audacity (2 pages)

RETURN TO PLENARY (page 31)

Starting to compose

OBJECTIVES

By the end of the lesson pupils should:

- develop an understanding of composing within a given framework inspired by traditional West African structures;
- begin to explore ways of notating and evaluating their work.

OUTCOMES

Pupils:

- compose a rhythm piece within a given composition framework using structures such as signals and cyclic patterns;
- represent their ideas through graphic and/or rhythm grid notation;
- use self and peer evaluation to assess their work in progress.

RESOURCES

CD-ROM
- Presentation
- Printouts 4, 17–23
- Video clips 8–10
- Teacher information (optional)

INSTRUMENTS
- Bells and shakers (or other available hand-held percussion)
- Variety of drums tuned to high, middle and low pitches (ideally a set of dunun drums and djembés)
- Beaters for dunun drums and bells
- Tuned instruments
- Electronic keyboards (optional)

ICT
- Whiteboard or computer and data projector with sound
- Audacity installed (optional)
- Recording equipment (optional)

PREPARATION

- Decide whether your pupils will work towards a performance of *Djolé* or compose their own rhythm piece.
- Set up a computer for pupils to record using Audacity (optional).

Printout 4: Learning intentions lessons 1–6

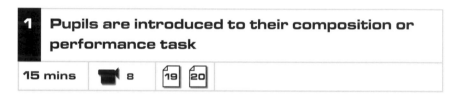

Focus			
5 mins	[4] [18]	**Presentation**	

- Make up a set of *Performance cards* (printout 18). Allocate individual cards to different groups to perform the musical task using voices or body percussion.

- Discuss the learning intentions for this lesson using the presentation on the CD-ROM or printout 4.

1	**Pupils are introduced to their composition or performance task**
15 mins	🎥 8 [19] [20]

- In advance of the lesson, decide whether your pupils will:

  · compose their own rhythm piece in groups and fulfil the criteria set out on printout 19;

  or

  · work towards a group performance of the rhythm piece, *Djolé*, and fulfil the criteria set out on printout 20.

- Introduce the composition or performance task to the pupils using printout 19 or 20 and go through the assessment criteria. Those composing their own rhythm pieces will be expected to:

  · invent their own main rhythm section comprising dunun and djembé cyclic patterns;

  · add structure to their composition by incorporating additional compositional ideas such as a signal, a call and response section or a break;

  · demonstrate their understanding of the compositional process, as applied to this genre.

For the group performance the pupils will be expected to:

  · develop their fluency in playing the rhythm piece, *Djolé,* with the song, *Laïlaïko*;

  · add structure to their performance by incorporating additional compositional ideas such as a break or call and response section;

  · work towards a polished performance and demonstrate an understanding of the genre.

TEACHING TIP

The following lessons will focus more on helping pupils compose their own cyclic pieces, as this is the more complex of the two tasks. If your pupils are working towards a performance of **Djolé**, it will still be relevant to work through most of the activities in the following lessons, but you may prefer to cover the activities in a little less detail to allow pupils time to practise for their performance.

■ Discuss the range of musical ideas that could be used as starting points for a composition.
(Ideas could include rhythms previously learnt during the unit or drawn from other musical genres or developed through improvisation.)

■ All watch video clip 8 to see how composer Tobias Stürmer creates the starting point for his piece, a polyrhythm created out of interlocking dunun and bell cyclic patterns.

■ Divide the class into small groups to start work on their own compositions. They should spend some time inventing and rehearsing their own dunun cyclic pattern/s. Suggest they:
  • try out their ideas using only voices and body percussion at first;
  • make sure their ideas are not too complicated as this is just the starting point;
  • explore fitting two or three rhythmic ideas together;
  • start to experiment with their ideas on instruments of their choice, once they are satisfied with how the ideas fit together.

TEACHING TIP

Pupils working towards a performance of the rhythm piece, **Djolé**, should first of all allocate the different parts amongst the group. They have already learnt the rhythms in previous lessons, but need to work together to make sure they are playing them accurately. Encourage them to start with the dunun cyclic patterns at a slow tempo.

Printout 18: Performance cards

Printout 19: Composition assessment criteria (2 pages)

Printout 20: Performance assessment criteria (2 pages)

2 Pupils develop and practise the main rhythm section for their piece

KEYBOARD page 38   **ICT** page 40

15 mins   🎥 9   [21] [22]

■ Each group performs their dunun cyclic pattern starting point to the class. Invite pupils from other groups to offer feedback. Suggest they think about:
  • how the rhythms combine to create an effective and interesting polyrhythm;
  • whether there is a steady pulse;
  • whether all group members are clear about what they are playing.

■ Watch video clip 9 to see how Tobias Stürmer develops his composition from the starting point of the dunun cyclic patterns. Discuss how he takes the composition forward:
  • he composes a signal;
  • he composes a djembé cyclic pattern to perform over the dunun and bell cyclic patterns;
  • he asks the lead drummer to improvise in the gaps between the beats played by the djembés;
  • he puts all this together and decides that it is his 'A section' or 'main groove'.

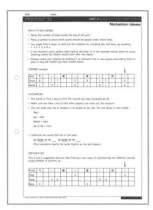

Printout 21: Notation ideas

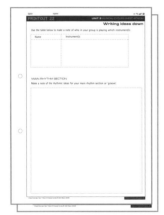

Printout 22: Writing ideas down (2 pages)

■ Pupils return to their groups to expand their own musical starting points into an 'A section' or 'main groove'.

■ Encourage pupils to start noting down their ideas. Distribute copies of printouts 21 and 22. Printout 21 suggests ways to notate rhythms and printout 22 provides space for the pupils to write ideas down.

TEACHING TIPS

You may wish to invite one or two groups to show work in progress regularly in order to keep the focus on the composition task and provide pupils with a range of good examples.

Make sure that the main rhythm section includes two or three interlocking cyclic patterns so that the music is polyrhythmic.

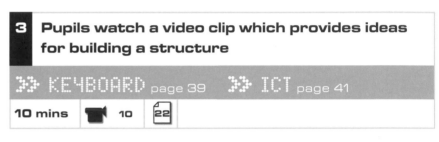

3 Pupils watch a video clip which provides ideas for building a structure

KEYBOARD page 39   ICT page 41

10 mins   10   22

■ Each group performs their work in progress. Those composing should have ideas in place for the main rhythm section of their piece. Those performing should have practised starting and stopping with a signal and playing the dunun and djembé cyclic patterns fluently. Invite individuals to offer feedback for each performance.

■ Explain that the pupils now need to build more of a structure for their piece. Explain the term **structure**.

■ Watch video clip 10 to see how Tobias Stürmer explores more ideas and begins to build a structure for his composition. Discuss the steps he takes, eg:

• he invents a rhythmic phrase which will become a break in the piece. Explain the term **break**;

• he composes a call and response section in which the master drummer improvises and the other players perform a composed response;

• he decides that the structure of his composition will be: 'A section'; break; call and response section; repeat of the 'A section'.

■ Pupils return to their groups to discuss and note down ideas from the video clip which they would like to explore next lesson. They write their ideas down on printout 22.

EXTENSION ACTIVITY

Groups continue to work on their rhythm pieces and explore ideas for other structural elements such as a break, call and response section or ending.

Plenary

5 mins

- Ask those working towards a composition what they think makes a strong composition, drawing on their own work in progress if they can;
(*eg rhythmic or melodic phrases that are easy to remember; signals that are easy to follow; a strong, clear pulse holding the fabric of the music together; interconnecting rhythms that work well with each other; use of dynamics and changes in tempo to create variety for the listener, etc).*

- Ask those working towards a performance what they think makes a good performance, drawing on their own work in progress if they can;
(*eg attention to dynamics, changes in tempo for different sections, clear leadership of the group through musical signals, good eye contact, everyone concentrating, technical accuracy etc).*

Homework

- Pupils should summarise their work so far in the space provided on printout 23. They should make a note of ideas for a final structure to bring to the next lesson to share with their group. (Suggest to pupils that they start work on this soon after the lesson in order that they do not forget their work so far.)

- Encourage pupils to bring in instruments from home next lesson as there will be an opportunity to integrate them into their composition or performance.

KEY WORDS

structure – how music is put together. This may refer to how a piece of music divides into sections, eg beginning, middle and end.

break – in West African music, a break is a short phrase played in unison by all performers, usually following a signal.

ASSESSMENT FOR LEARNING

Who can explain their ideas and contribute well to the group composition or performance process?

Who understands the given structure and works creatively within it?

Who uses notation and ICT to record their work in progress?

Printout 23: Homework:
ideas for rhythm piece

KEYBOARD (see page 35)

2 Pupils develop and practise the main rhythm section for their piece

15 mins 9

- Pupils perform and discuss their dunun cyclic pattern starting point, then watch video clip 9 which shows how Tobias Stürmer develops his starting point to create an 'A section' or 'main groove', see page 35.

- Pupils return to their groups to expand their own musical starting points into an 'A section' or 'main groove'.

- Encourage those using keyboards to:
  - revise the voices selected in lessons 1 and 2 when they learnt the cyclic patterns for *Djolé* ;
  - set an audible steady pulse on the keyboard using the metronome, or recording their own steady pulse into the keyboard using a bell or agogo voice;
  - transfer their musical starting points to the keyboard sounds;
  - record the dunun cyclic patterns for the 'main groove' into the keyboard memory, repeating each one at least eight times;
  - play the recordings back and experiment with how other rhythms might fit into and around it in the same way that the djembé rhythms fit with the dunun rhythms in *Djolé*;
  - explore different timbres for a new cyclic pattern and play it together with the dunun cyclic patterns.

- Encourage pupils to start noting down their ideas and suggest the order they might come in. Distribute copies of printouts 21 and 22. Printout 21 suggests ways to notate rhythms and printout 22 provides space for the pupils to write ideas down.

TEACHING TIPS

Encourage groups to share their work with each other.

Make sure that the main rhythm section, or 'A section' includes two or three interlocking cyclic patterns so that the music is polyrhythmic.

If keyboards are limited in their multi-tracking facility, encourage pupils to work in larger groups so that they are able to perform all their dunun and djembé cyclic patterns on keyboards, even if they perform the additional ideas using body percussion and vocalisation.

◀◀ RETURN TO ACTIVITY 3 (page 36)

KEYBOARD 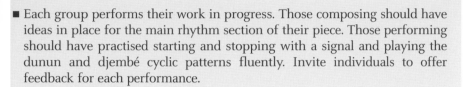 (see page 36)

3 **Pupils watch a video clip which provides ideas for building a structure**

10 mins 10   21 22

- Each group performs their work in progress. Those composing should have ideas in place for the main rhythm section of their piece. Those performing should have practised starting and stopping with a signal and playing the dunun and djembé cyclic patterns fluently. Invite individuals to offer feedback for each performance.

- Explain that the pupils now need to build more of a structure for their piece. Explain the term **structure**.

- Watch video clip 10 to see how Tobias Stürmer explores more ideas and begins to build a structure for his composition. Discuss the steps he takes, as described on page 36.

- Pupils return to their groups to discuss and note down ideas from the video clip which they would like to explore next lesson. Encourage those using keyboards to:

  - explore ideas using voices or body percussion first;
  - listen again to any tracks recorded into their keyboard memory and consider what might come after it, with it or before it;
  - write down all their ideas on printout 22 (using printout 21 for support, if required), including keeping a note of any different voice sounds to remember for next lesson;
  - record their work in progress to disk, if their keyboard has this facility.

EXTENSION ACTIVITY

Groups continue to work on their rhythm pieces and explore ideas for other structural elements such as a break, call and response section or ending. Encourage those using keyboards to record ideas onto a separate track and then experiment with where and when to bring them in.

◀◀ RETURN TO PLENARY   (page 37)

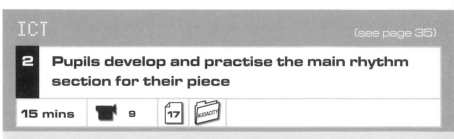

ICT   (see page 35)

**2   Pupils develop and practise the main rhythm
        section for their piece**

15 mins   🎥 9   [17]   📁 AUDACITY

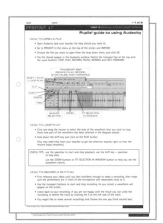

Printout 17: Pupils' guide to
using Audacity (2 pages)

- Before the lesson, make sure that a computer is set up to record using Audacity. (See *Using Audacity* in the Teacher information section of the CD-ROM for information on how to do this).

- Pupils perform and discuss their starting points and then watch video clip 9 which shows how Tobias Stürmer develops his starting point to create an 'A section' or 'main groove', see page 35.

- Pupils return to their groups to expand their own musical starting points into an 'A section' or 'main groove'.

- One group works with ICT using Audacity and a copy of the *Pupils' guide to using Audacity* (printout 17). They should:
  - choose one rhythm they have devised using voices and body percussion to record (they may decide that the whole group performs the rhythm together in unison, or that one person performs for the recording);
  - make a recording of the rhythm performed four times;
  - save their recording, once they are satisfied with it, as an Audacity project with an appropriate file name;
  - play back the recording and choose one repetition of the rhythm to loop (one that was performed well);
  - carefully select the appropriate area of the waveform, and then loop play the rhythm as a cyclic pattern;
  - check the rhythm loops smoothly, then use the TRIM function to delete everything recorded except the looped rhythm;
  - save the file again.

TEACHING TIPS

The group using ICT will need to work near to the computer where they can hear the computer's sound system and see the screen. Check that playback can be heard clearly.

Make sure pupils know the basic operations on Audacity, how to: play, stop, record and delete a track. One person in the group should be in charge of these tasks initially.

They may need several 'takes' to get a reasonable recording. Unsatisfactory tracks should be deleted immediately to avoid confusion.

When selecting the area of the recording to loop, pupils may need to resize the waveform so that they can see clearly the area they want to loop.

Remind pupils that they can use the UNDO function if any trim or delete operation goes wrong.

- The group then experiments with one or two contrasting patterns to perform over the looped rhythm, so as to develop a 'main groove' for their piece that incorporates their recording.

◀◀ RETURN TO ACTIVITY 3   (page 36)

ICT  (see page 36)

3 **Pupils watch a video clip which provides ideas for building a structure**

10 mins 10

■ Each group performs their work in progress. Those composing should have ideas in place for the main rhythm section of their piece. Those performing should have practised starting and stopping with a signal and playing the dunun and djembé cyclic patterns fluently. Invite individuals to offer feedback for each performance.

■ Explain that the pupils now need to build more of a structure for their piece. Explain the term **structure**.

■ Watch video clip 10 to see how Tobias Stürmer explores more ideas and begins to build a structure for his composition. Discuss the steps he takes, as described on page 36.

■ Pupils return to their groups to discuss and note down ideas from the video clip which they would like to explore next lesson. They write their ideas down on printout 22 (using printout 21 for support, if required). Encourage those using ICT to:

• think about how many times they will repeat their recorded rhythm as the basis for their 'A section' or 'main groove';

• record a couple of ideas into Audacity to remember for next lesson;

• discuss the advantages and disadvantages of using ICT for this piece of work.

TEACHING TIPS

One person in the group could be assigned the task of tapping the spacebar to start and stop the loop in time with the performance. This person could then perform a simpler part such as the steady pulse.

 **RETURN** TO PLENARY (page 37)

Lesson 5   Developing and rehearsing

OBJECTIVES

By the end of the lesson pupils should:

- have improved and developed their composition or performance;

- have begun to plan the way in which they wish their music to be performed;

- continue to notate and begin to record their work.

OUTCOMES

Pupils:

- represent their ideas through graphic and/or rhythm grid notation;

- work as a group to evaluate their composition or performance so far.

RESOURCES

AUDIO CD
Tracks 36–37

CD-ROM
- Presentation
- Printouts 4, 15, 17, 19–23
- Video clip 11
- Teacher information (optional)

INSTRUMENTS
- Bells and shakers (or other available hand-held percussion)
- Variety of drums tuned to high, middle and low pitches (ideally a set of dunun drums and djembés)
- Beaters for dunun drums and bells
- Tuned instruments
- Electronic keyboards (optional)

ICT
- Whiteboard or computer and data projector with sound
- Audacity installed (optional)
- Recording equipment (optional)

Focus						
10 mins	🎥 11	4	19	20	**Presentation**	

- Watch the performance of Tobias Stürmer's rhythm piece, *Djembé jam* (video clip 11). Discuss:

  - which structural and musical elements he has chosen to use;
    (signal, cyclic patterns, break, call and response, improvisation, ending)

  - how the second rhythm section is different from the first;
    (it is faster and louder and the improvised passages are extended)

  - how he brought the piece to an end;
    (by using the same break as he used at the end of the first rhythm section with the dunun drums joining in on the last two notes)

  - how he used changes in dynamics and tempo to help build the piece;
    (there is a marked change during the call and response section from a soft and slow mood to a stronger and more energetic mood)

  - any other aspects of the performance.
    (eg all the performers were moving in time with the music; they all looked to be enjoying themselves; there was good eye contact between performers.)

- Discuss the learning intentions for this lesson using the presentation on the CD-ROM or printout 4, and revise the assessment criteria (printouts 19 and 20).

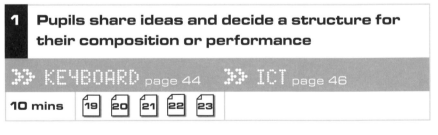

1	**Pupils share ideas and decide a structure for their composition or performance**

>> KEYBOARD page 44   **>> ICT** page 46

10 mins	19	20	21	22	23

Printout 4: Learning intentions lessons 1–6

- Each group revises their work from last lesson and shares ideas from their homework. They try out as many ideas as possible and decide a final structure for their composition or version of *Djolé*. They should think about:

  - how the piece will start and finish;

  - which other structural elements they will use, eg break or call and response;

  - who will improvise and in which sections;

  - what the overall tempo and dynamics of the piece will be.

TEACHING TIPS

Pupils should have a copy of printouts 19 or 20 and 21–22 to hand as they work.

Those working towards a performance should additionally think about when and how they will include the song, *Laïlaïko*, and about changes in tempo and/or dynamics.

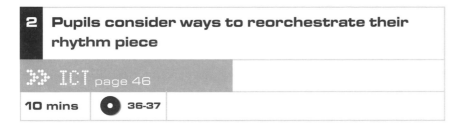

2 Pupils consider ways to reorchestrate their rhythm piece

ICT page 46

10 mins ● 36-37

- Listen to tracks 36 and 37 to hear how Tobias Stürmer reorchestrated his rhythm piece, *Djembé jam*, into *Djembé funk*, a composition for drum kit, bongos, tambourine, electric bass guitar, keyboard pad, electric piano, electric guitar, trumpet, timbales and synthesizer. Discuss:

  - how melodic instruments can be used to play cyclic patterns;
    (eg a dunun rhythm can be transferred on to electric bass guitar)
  - how other percussion instruments can be used to add atmosphere;
    (eg cymbal rolls from the drum kit)
  - how pupils' existing compositions or performances could be enhanced or developed by the use of different timbres.
    (eg replacing one timbre for another, or introducing new timbres into the piece, such as instruments pupils could bring in from home.)

- Pupils consider how they might include melodic instruments in their performance or composition. Suggest they use notes from the pentatonic scale A C D E G. They might also like to use instruments they have brought in from home.

3 Pupils refine and rehearse their composition or version of Djolé

KEYBOARD page 45   **ICT** page 47

15 mins 21 22

- Each group spends time refining and rehearsing their rhythm pieces. Pupils may wish to reorchestrate some parts of their composition or add other instruments to the ensemble.

- By the end of the lesson pupils should make sure they:

  - can play through their entire piece from start to finish;
  - have made a note of the structure of their piece and all the different rhythmic or melodic components on printout 22;
  - have made a note of any additional decisions they have made, eg use of dynamics, who is improvising in each section, etc.

TEACHING TIPS

You may wish to regularly invite one or two groups to show work in progress in order to keep the focus on the composition task and provide pupils with a range of good examples.

Make sure pupils have a copy of *Notation ideas* (printout 21), if required.

As you circulate, listen to work in progress and offer assistance where required. Encourage any groups who are struggling to simplify their structure.

Printout 19: Composition assessment criteria (2 pages)

Printout 20: Performance assessment criteria (2 pages)

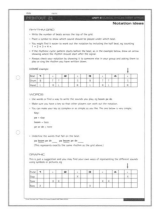

Printout 21: Notation ideas

Printout 22: Writing ideas down (2 pages)

ASSESSMENT FOR LEARNING

Who can vocalise or describe their ideas?

Who contributes well to their group's work?

Who understands the given structure and works creatively within it?

Who uses notation and ICT to record their work in progress?

Plenary	
5 mins	

- As a class, discuss pupils thoughts on using reorchestration to access West African music.

- Ask pupils whether they prefer the authentic instruments used in *Djembé jam* or the instruments used in *Djembé funk*.

- Discuss the difference between playing and feeling a rhythm on a drum and producing the same rhythm using keyboards or ICT. Why might both routes have advantages?

Homework

- Ask each pupil to write a review (one paragraph only) of *Djembé funk* as if for a music magazine. They should make sure they:

  · explain how they think the piece fits together;

  · discuss the composer's choice of instruments in his reorchestration.

KEYBOARD (see page 42)

1 Pupils share ideas and decide a structure for their composition or performance

10 mins [19] [20] [21] [22] [23]

- Each group revises their work from last lesson and shares their ideas from their homework (printout 23). They should try out as many of the ideas as possible and decide upon a final structure for their performance or composition. Those using keyboards should:

  · revise the main section's interlocking cyclic patterns to make sure these are recorded and accessible, or that everyone is confident playing them.

  · if the keyboard has the facility, record the different cyclic patterns into different tracks in the keyboard;

  · decide how the piece will start and finish;

  · decide which other structural elements they will use, eg breaks, call and response sections and an ending and choose appropriate timbres;

  · listen to their recorded tracks again and think about how to cross smoothly from one section into another;

  · decide who will improvise and in which sections;

  · decide what the overall tempo and dynamics of the piece will be;

  · ensure that ideas and timbres are noted down, and if possible recorded to disk;

  · have a copy of printout 19 or 20 and 21–22 to hand as they work.

 **RETURN** TO ACTIVITY 2 (page 43)

KEYBOARD

(see page 43)

3 **Pupils refine and rehearse their composition or version of Djolé**

15 mins 15 21 22

■ Each group spends time refining and rehearsing their rhythm pieces. Pupils may wish to reorchestrate some parts of their composition or performance or add other instruments to the ensemble. Encourage those using keyboards to:

- think about how Tobias Stürmer introduced the bass guitar for the dunun cyclic patterns, and explore the different bass sounds on their keyboard;
- choose one bass timbre for each of their dunun cyclic patterns and transfer the rhythm pattern to pitched notes, using pitches taken from the pentatonic scale A C D E and G;
- record the new version, then listen back and compare their original with their reorchestrated version and consider which they think an audience would prefer and why;
- consider whether they wish to use both ideas in their final composition or performance;
- think about whether to include pitch for any other sections of their rhythm piece.

■ Pupils make a note of any changes on printout 22. By the end of the lesson pupils should make sure they:

- can play through their entire piece from start to finish;
- have made a note of the structure of their piece and all the different rhythmic or melodic components;
- have made a note on printout 22 of any additional decisions they have made, eg use of dynamics, who is improvising in each section, etc.

TEACHING TIPS

Make sure pupils have a copy of *Notation ideas* (printout 21), if required.

Those working towards a performance of *Djolé* should additionally think about when and how they will include the song, *Laïlaïko*. They may like to refer to *Laïlaïko melody: keyboard* (printout 15).

RETURN TO PLENARY (page 44)

Printout 15: Laïlaïko melody: keyboard

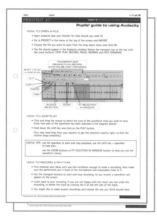

Printout 17: Pupils' guide to
using Audacity (2 pages)

ICT   (see page 42)

1 | **Pupils share ideas and decide a structure for their composition or performance**

10 mins | 17 19 20 21 22 23 AUDACITY

- The ICT group listens to the looped rhythm they recorded last lesson. Remind the pupils that this looped rhythm should be the basis for the 'A section' or 'main groove' of their composition or version of *Djolé*.

- Explain that in this lesson the pupils may like to record an additional track to play at the same time as their looped rhythm. Before they do this, they will need to copy and paste their existing rhythm to create a track to record with. They should therefore decide how many times to repeat the rhythm and then follow the instructions for copying and pasting on printout 17.

- The pupils revise the other ideas they noted down last lesson and share new ideas from their homework (printouts 21–23). They should try out as many ideas as possible and consider how they may best use their recordings as part of a live performance.

- Each group decides upon a final structure for their performance of *Djolé* or own composition, as described on page 42 and using printout 19 or 20 for support.

RETURN TO ACTIVITY 2   (page 43)

ICT   (see page 43)

2 | **Pupils consider ways to reorchestrate their rhythm piece**

10 mins | ● 36-37 AUDACITY

- Listen to tracks 36 and 37 and discuss how Tobias Stürmer reorchestrated his rhythm piece, *Djembé jam*, into *Djembé funk*, a composition for drum kit, bongos, tambourine, electric bass guitar, keyboard pad, electric piano, electric guitar, trumpet, timbales and synthesizer, as described on page 43.

- Each group considers how they might include additional instruments in their performance or composition. Those using ICT might consider recording a second track. To do this they should:

  - choose which rhythmic idea to record;
  - if transferring the rhythm onto a tuned instrument, consider using the pentatonic scale A C D E G;
  - decide which instrument to use, who will play it, and who will operate the computer;
  - practise the new idea until it is secure.

RETURN TO ACTIVITY 3   (page 43)

ICT   (see page 43)

| **2** | **Pupils refine and rehearse their composition or version of Djolé** |

15 mins   [AUDACITY]

- Each group spends time refining and rehearsing their composition or version of *Djolé*.

- Those using ICT should first make a recording of the new part they practised in activity 2 (following the guidance in the *Pupils' guide to using Audacity*, printout 17).

- The ICT group will be using a combination of recorded tracks and live instruments. To help them build their rhythm piece they will need to:

  - decide when to add live playing while a file is playing in Audacity, such as additional cyclic patterns and improvisation;
  - decide when to have no file playing in Audacity, for example in a break or call and response section involving the whole group;
  - decide which ideas work well together and evaluate their work as they go along.

- By the end of the lesson, those using ICT should:

  - have worked out how to incorporate playing live instruments and recorded tracks in their composition or performance;
  - be able to play through their entire piece from start to finish;
  - have made a note of the structure of their piece on printout 22.

TEACHING TIPS

If pupils want to listen to one track in Audacity while they record another, they need to make sure the sound output from the PC is loud enough for the performers to hear the rhythm track, but not so loud that it is recorded again on the new track via the microphone. If possible, the pupil playing the instrument can use headphones while recording.

Make sure pupils have a copy of *Notation ideas* (printout 21) if required.

EXTENSION ACTIVITY

Encourage groups that are working confidently and successfully with Audacity to experiment with and develop their recording further, eg:

- use the SOLO and MUTE buttons on each track to affect changes of texture without stopping the playback;
- create a 'permanent mute' by selecting part of a track, for example, two repetitions of the cyclic rhythm, and silencing it (go to the EDIT menu, then select SILENCE);
- record more tracks;
- go to the EFFECTS menu to change the timbre of a sound, eg try echo, phaser, or wah wah.

RETURN TO PLENARY   (page 44)

OBJECTIVES

By the end of the lesson pupils should:

- be able to perform **Djolé** or their own composition to the rest of the class;
- be able to appraise their own work and the work of other groups;

OUTCOMES

Pupils:

- perform **Djolé** or their own composition to the class;
- identify and evaluate the musical ideas within their own work and the work of others and how they fit together;
- evaluate their work.

RESOURCES

CD-ROM
- Presentation
- Printouts 1, 4, 19–20, 24
- Teacher information (optional)

INSTRUMENTS
- Bells and shakers (or other available hand-held percussion)
- Variety of drums tuned to high, middle and low pitches (ideally a set of dunun drums and djembés)
- Beaters for dunun drums and bells
- Tuned instruments
- Electronic keyboards (optional)

ICT
- Whiteboard or computer and data projector with sound
- Audacity installed (optional)
- Recording equipment (optional)

Printout 4: Learning intentions lessons 1–6

Printout 19: Composition assessment criteria (2 pages)

Focus			
5 mins	[4] [19] [20]	**Presentation**	

- Discuss the learning intentions for this lesson using the presentation on the CD-ROM or printout 4.

- Discuss the reviews of **Djembé funk** the pupils wrote for homework, and discuss whether this activity has made anyone think more critically about their own rhythm piece.

- Review the assessment criteria (printouts 19 and 20) for this unit and discuss how the different levels can be met.

1 Pupils rehearse their composition or version of Djolé in their groups

KEYBOARD page 50   **ICT** page 50

10 mins

- Each group spends ten minutes practising their version of **Djolé** or their own composition to perform to the class. Encourage them to:

  - practise at a slower tempo to get the rhythms under their fingers;
  - remember to vary the dynamics and tempo if possible;
  - think about how to group the players to ensure good eye contact and communication with the audience;
  - make sure there is a clear leadership in the group;
  - make sure that everyone knows how to start and stop and can move smoothly from one section to the next.

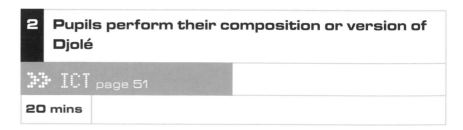

2 Pupils perform their composition or version of Djolé

ICT page 51

20 mins

- Each group performs their version of the rhythm piece, **Djolé**, or their own composition to the class. Encourage the class to think about and feed back on:

- which rhythmic or melodic ideas are easy to remember;
- which cyclic patterns work well with each other;
- whether the signals are easy to follow;
- whether there is a strong, clear pulse holding the music together;
- whether the group makes good use of dynamics and tempo to create variety for the listener.

TEACHING TIPS

You may wish to record each group's work to support further evaluation. You could use Audacity to do this (see *Using Audacity* in the Teacher information section of the CD-ROM).

For those performing their version of the rhythm piece, *Djolé*, you might like to video the performance so pupils can evaluate their own performances.

For those using keyboards, encourage the class to additionally think about whether or not the keyboard players have chosen convincing timbres.

3 | Evaluate and assess the performances

>> KEYBOARD page 51   >> ICT page 51

10 mins | 19 | 20 |

- Pupils feed back verbally on what they thought was successful about each group's performance. They should consider:
  - how well members of the group communicated with each other;
  - which musical ideas worked well;
  - which musical ideas were the most impressive;
  - how well the players performed in time with each other and the steady pulse.

- Pupils then work in their own groups with a copy of the assessment criteria (printouts 19 or 20). They discuss the level they consider their performance or composition to be and identify anything they would change next time.

- Each group feeds back to the rest of the class.

Plenary

5 mins | 1 | 24 | **Presentation**

- Remind pupils of the learning intentions for this unit using the presentation on the CD-ROM or printout 1.

- Discuss what the class has enjoyed learning about most in this unit.

- Distribute copies of the *End of unit evaluation sheet* (printout 24) and discuss how the pupils should complete it for homework.

 **Homework** | 24 |

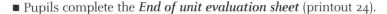

- Pupils complete the *End of unit evaluation sheet* (printout 24).

ASSESSMENT FOR LEARNING

Who is able to make a clear summary of evidence to match the assessment criteria?

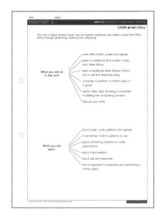

Printout 20: Performance assessment criteria (2 pages)

Printout 1: Unit overview

Printout 24: End of unit evaluation sheet (2 pages)

KEYBOARD (see page 48)

1 **Pupils rehearse their composition or version of Djolé in their groups**

10 mins

■ The keyboard group spends ten minutes practising their version of *Djolé* or their own composition to perform to the class. Encourage them to:

- practise at a slower tempo to get the rhythms under their fingers;
- make sure there is a clear leadership in the group;
- make sure that everyone knows how to start and stop and can move smoothly from one section to the next;
- ensure that they are clear which sections of the performance or composition will involve accessing pre-recorded work or work on disk, and which sections will be performed live;
- have a list of voice numbers to hand if different timbres are required during the piece;
- make sure somebody is in charge of changing the volume of the different sections, if required;
- work out clear physical cues for pupils playing side by side at the keyboard where eye contact is difficult.

RETURN TO ACTIVITY 2 (page 48)

ICT (see page 48)

1 **Pupils rehearse their composition or version of Djolé in their groups**

10 mins

■ The ICT group spends ten minutes practising their version of *Djolé* or their own composition to perform to the class. Encourage them to:

- practise at a slower tempo to get the rhythms under their fingers;
- remember to vary the dynamics and tempo if possible;
- make sure there is a clear leadership in the group;
- make sure that everyone knows how to start and stop and can move smoothly and in time from one section to the next;
- make sure each person understands their role, whether performing an instrument or operating the computer;
- ensure the group are arranged so as to maintain eye contact with each other and the audience;
- check that volume levels are balanced between live and acoustic sounds.

RETURN TO ACTIVITY 2 (page 48)

ICT   (see page 48)

2 Pupils perform their composition or version of Djolé

20 mins

■ Each group performs their version of the rhythm piece, *Djolé*, or their own composition to the class. Encourage the class to think about and feed back on:

- which rhythmic or melodic ideas are easy to remember;
- which cyclic patterns work well with each other;
- whether the signals are easy to follow;
- whether there is a strong, clear pulse holding the music together;
- whether the group makes good use of dynamics and tempo to create variety for the listener.

■ For those performing using ICT, ask the class to also consider:

- in what ways ICT has added to the quality of the group's piece and helped them to complete the task;
- how ICT may have held the group back in their work or compromised the quality of their final piece.

RETURN TO ACTIVITY 3   (page 49)

KEYBOARD/ICT   (see page 49)

3 Evaluate and assess the performances

10 mins

■ Each group evaluates and assesses their performance and then feeds back to the class (see page 49).

■ As they do this, the keyboard and ICT groups should also consider how the use of keyboards or ICT contributed to the success of their work. They might draw on, for example:

- the strong energetic quality of the looped rhythms;
- the stable, metronome-like pulse;
- the ability to layer tracks helps to create a structure.

They should also consider how using keyboards or ICT may have been less effective. They might have found, for example:

- that they were less able to be spontaneous when performing;
- that they were not able to change tempo;
- that they had difficulties playing an acoustic instrument over a recorded rhythm.

RETURN TO PLENARY   (page 49)

Djolé: dunun cyclic patterns

Symbols

X = bell

O = Open drum (beater bouncing off the centre of the drum skin)
C = Closed drum (beater held firmly against the drum skin)

Full cyclic patterns:

Dununba (low bass drum)

Pulse	1				2				3				4			
bell	X		X	X		X	X		X		X	X		X	X	
drum	O								O							

Sangban (middle bass drum)

Pulse	1				2				3				4			
bell	X		X		X		X		X		X		X		X	
drum	C				O				C				O			

Kenkeni (high bass drum)

Pulse	1				2				3				4			
bell			X	X		X	X			X	X		X	X		
drum			O	O		O	O			O	O		O	O		

Simplified cyclic patterns:

Dununba (low bass drum)

Pulse	1				2				3				4			
bell			X		X		X				X		X		X	
drum	O								O							

Sangban (middle bass drum)

Pulse	1				2				3				4			
bell	X		X			X	X		X						X	
drum						O								O		

Kenkeni (high bass drum)

Pulse	1				2				3				4			
bell	X				X				X				X			
drum			O				O				O				O	

Djolé: signal and djembé cyclic patterns

Signal

4			1	+	2	+	3	+	4	+	
(X) optional			X	X	X	X	X	X	X	X	X

Symbols

B = bass
T = tone
S = slap
R / L = right or left hand
(for the simplified parts, these are only suggestions, play what feels most comfortable).

Full cyclic patterns:

Djembé 1

Pulse	1				2				3				4			
Drum	B		T	T	B	S	S	B	T	T	B	S	S			
Hands	R		R	L	R	R	L	R	R	L	R	R	L			

Djembé 2

Pulse	1				2				3				4			
Drum	B			T	T			B				T	T	T	T	
Hands	R			L	R			R				R	L	R	L	

Pulse	5				6				7				8			
Drum	T			T	T			B				T				
Hands	R			L	R			R				R				

Simplified cyclic patterns:

Djembé 1

Pulse	1				2				3				4			
Drum	B		T	T	B			B	T	T	B					
Hands	R		R	L	R			R	R	L	R					

Djembé 2

Pulse	1				2				3				4			
Drum	B				B				B				T	T	T	T
Hands	R				L				R				R	L	R	L

GLOSSARY

break	In West African music, a break is a short phrase played in unison by all performers, usually following a signal.
call and response	A type of song in which a soloist sings a phrase which is then responded to by a larger group of singers.
cyclic pattern	A musical pattern that repeats continuously. Cyclic patterns may be rhythmic or melodic.
djembé	A solo or lead drum made from a single piece of wood shaped like a goblet with a playing head made from goat skin. The djembé is a Mandinka drum.
dunun	A Mandinka bass drum often played in a set of three different sizes, each with a bell, to accompany the djembé. Sometimes also known as *djun djun* or *doundoun*.
dununba	The largest dunun (see dunun).
dynamics	The volume at which music is played.
improvisation	A performance created as it is played.
kenkeni	The smallest dunun (see dunun).
lead drummer	A drummer who directs the rest of the ensemble and any dancers by providing musical signals and solo improvisations.
Mandinka	A West African ethnic group and language. Sometimes also known as Malinké or Mandingue, the Mandinka people live in countries such as Guinea, Mali, Burkina Faso, Senegal and The Gambia.
master drummer	A drummer acknowledged by other musicians and members of the community to have complete technical mastery and a thorough understanding of the drum, its music and its culture.
mnemonic	A word or sound used to remind a player which hand to use or note to play. Not used traditionally in any systematic sense by djembé players, but is more characteristic of some Ghanaian drumming.
pentatonic scale	A five-note scale.
phrase	A section of a larger melody.
pitch	The complete range of sounds in music from the highest to the lowest. A general rule of thumb in music is the larger the instrument, the lower its pitch.
polyrhythm	More than one rhythm played at the same time.
pulse	A steady beat.
rhythm patterns	Combinations of different note lengths organised into patterns.
sangban	The mid-sized dunun (see dunun).